What people are sayin  T0002141

Quaker Quicks — Open to New Light

Open to New Light covers a huge amount of ground in an accessible way, in a short space, without making the material seem in any way simplistic or superficial. I am sure the book will be received as a very valuable introduction to the topic.
Stuart Masters, Programme Coordinator (History and Theology), Woodbrooke, Birmingham, UK

Nesbitt provides an accessible and deeply informed account of Quakers engaged in interfaith activity over the last three and a half centuries. This is not purely a historian's view, but that of a practitioner, who lives out her own interfaith quest. Nesbitt's spirit is gentle and open, her writing incisive, always aware of complexities and questions, always searching for a deeper truth to find equality, justice, community, simplicity and peace. I am not a Quaker. I found so much to learn from this book and commend it to all engaged reflectively with interfaith matters.
Gavin D'Costa, Emeritus Professor of Catholic Theology, University of Bristol; Professor of Interreligious Dialogue, Pontifical University of St Thomas Aquinas, Rome

A Quaker by convincement who has herself been involved in interfaith explorations, Eleanor Nesbitt has given us a well-researched and highly accessible account of liberal Quaker (Society of Friends) encounters with other faith traditions over the past 350 years.
As a follow up to her *Interfaith Pilgrims* (2003), Nesbitt explores how liberal Friends from Britain and North America, pursuing a Quaker approach of 'discerning openness', have interacted with peoples of non-Christian religions (Baha'i, Buddhist, Hindu,

Jain, Muslim, Sikh, Pagan, and humanist) – in their travels, commonly exhibiting a readiness 'to learn from others' and 'to work with other communities of faith' and, at home, following 'an imperative of being a good neighbour to newcomers from different faith backgrounds'.

Nesbitt also provides us with accounts of how Friends have themselves come to be viewed by members of these other religious traditions, discusses cases of individuals who have taken on merged identities (as, for example, 'Muslim Quaker' or 'Buddhist Quaker' or 'Hindu Quaker'), and explores various Quaker interfaith initiatives.

Open to New Light exhibits Nesbitt's personal and scholarly familiarity with Quakerism as well as her personal and scholarly familiarity with other religious traditions. (She is married to a Hindu and is herself a leading Sikh studies scholar.) This background makes for a book both heartfelt and knowledgeable and one that should be of interest to Quakers and non-Quakers alike.

Verne A. Dusenbery, Professor Emeritus of Anthropology, Hamline University, USA

Eleanor Nesbitt offers a compelling, meticulous and insightful historical account of Quaker interfaith journey focusing on the seventeenth and eighteenth centuries as well as later and contemporary developments in Quaker thought and interreligious engagement. *Open to New Light* encompasses a wide range of religious faiths and indigenous traditions that Quakers, of varying theological orientations, have interacted with over the last 350 years and shows how both Quakers and adherents of diverse faiths have been deeply enriched by their interfaith encounters in different contexts. What comes across clearly in Quaker interfaith engagement is their commitment to 'values of truth and integrity equality and justice, community, simplicity and peace' and their openness and willingness to see

'God in everyone' and 'God in everything'. This book should be of enormous interest not only to Quakers but also to those of other faiths or none.

Sharada Sugirtharajah, Honorary Senior Research Fellow, School of Philosophy, Theology and Religion, University of Birmingham

Previous books

Listening to Hindus (with Robert Jackson) Unwin Hyman, 1990 ISBN 0 04 448121 7

Hindu Children in Britain (with Robert Jackson) Trentham Books, 1993 ISBN 0 948080 736

Guru Nanak (with Gopinder Kaur) Bayeux Arts, 1999 ISBN 9781896209272, 1896209270

Interfaith Pilgrims, Quaker Books, 2003 ISBN 97809016 89931

Intercultural Education: Ethnographic and religious approaches, Sussex Academic Press, 2004 ISBN 978 1 84519 034 7

Sikhism A Very Short Introduction, Oxford University Press, 2005; 2nd revised edn 2016 ISBN 978 0 19 874557 0

Pool of Life: The autobiography of a Punjabi agony aunt (with Kailash Puri), Sussex Academic Press, 2013 978 1 84519 602 8

Making Nothing Happen: Five poets explore faith and spirituality (with Gavin D'Costa, Mark Pryce, Ruth Shelton and Nicola Slee) Ashgate, 2014 ISBN 978 1 4094 5515 8

Sikh: Two centuries of western women's art and writing, Kashi House, 2022 ISBN 1911271202

Quaker Quicks — Open to New Light

Quakers and Other Faiths

Quaker Quicks — Open to New Light

Quakers and Other Faiths

Eleanor Nesbitt

CHRISTIAN ALTERNATIVE
BOOKS

Winchester, UK
Washington, USA

JOHN HUNT PUBLISHING

First published by Christian Alternative Books, 2023
Christian Alternative Books is an imprint of John Hunt Publishing Ltd.,
No. 3 East St., Alresford, Hampshire SO24 9EE, UK
office@jhpbooks.com
www.johnhuntpublishing.com
www.christian-alternative.com

For distributor details and how to order please visit the 'Ordering' section on our website.

ISBN: 978 1 80341 323 5
978 1 80341 324 2 (ebook)
Library of Congress Control Number: 2022947204

A CIP catalogue record for this book is available from the British Library.

Design: Lapiz Digital Services

UK: Printed and bound by CPI Group (UK) Ltd, Croydon, CR0 4YY
Printed in North America by CPI GPS partners

To my friends in Coventry Quaker Meeting

Contents

Preface

This is a book for anyone who is interested in religions and the ways in which they have been interacting over the past three and a half centuries. The content will be of particular interest to Quakers but by no means only to Quakers.

Space constraints have limited what can be said here about faith communities and their religious beliefs and practices and about Quakers' relations with them. My reporting has necessarily focused on particular strands and particular periods – seventeenth-century encounters with Native Americans and pre-First World War correspondence between Baha'is and Quakers, for instance. The publications mentioned in the References provide ample sources of further information for the interested reader.

Whether you are a seasoned Friend, a well-travelled interfaith explorer or relatively new to the subject, I hope that you will find some stimulus to journey further. I welcome your views and reactions and so my contact details are included at the end of the book.

Eleanor Nesbitt
September 2022

Acknowledgments

Thank you to Jennifer Kavanagh for the initial push, and to Rex Ambler, to Wendy Burnett of Central England Area Meeting, as well as to Gopinder Kaur, Alison Mukherjee, Amarjit Singh and Satwinder Kaur for helpful comments. Many thanks to Gavin D'Costa, Verne A. Dusenbery, Stuart Masters and Sharada Sugirtharajah for their generous endorsements. I am especially grateful for support from Stella Roberts of Coventry Local Meeting and Murray Short of Aotearoa/New Zealand Yearly Meeting, and for vital help from both Bettina Gray and Stuart Masters at Woodbrooke Quaker Study Centre.

Abbreviations

CFP = *Christian Faith and Practice in the Experience of the Society of Friends* (1960) London: London Yearly Meeting of the Religious Society of Friends.

QFP = *Quaker Faith and Practice: The book of Christian discipline of the Yearly Meeting of the Religious Society of Friends (Quakers) in Britain*, 1995, London: The Yearly Meeting of the Religious Society of Friends (Quakers) in Britain.

CIRC = Christian Interfaith Relations Committee

QCCIR = Quaker Committee for Christian and Interfaith Relations

Chapter 1: Getting started

In following the story of Quakers' encounters and engagement with other faiths and their practitioners, readers are encouraged to consider whether the values of truth and integrity, equality and justice, community, simplicity, and peace (often referred to as Quaker testimonies) have contributed or, indeed, been a driving motivation. You are also urged (whatever your background, worldview or religious allegiance) to seek out any relevance in these encounters to your own interfaith explorations and initiatives.

I write 'interfaith' as a single, unhyphenated word even though I appreciate the viewpoint of those who would prefer 'inter faith' or 'inter-faith'. While respecting concerns for the separateness and distinctiveness of faiths I also recognise the surge in formal and informal interactions and the fluidity and plurality of many people's religious identities. Their (your) spirituality and sense of self may already be interfaith, drawing on multiple sources and caught up in an internal conversation.

For over 350 years Quakers (members of the Religious Society of Friends) have been interacting with people of diverse religious communities. Quakers (also known as Friends) have been coming across various religious beliefs and giving them serious thought. They have shared their own experiences and insights and, sometimes, they have mentioned what people of other faiths thought about Quakers' own behaviour and beliefs. Occasionally, too, Quakers are mentioned appraisingly in the reflections of Muslims and Jews, Hindus, Buddhists, Sikhs, Baha'is, Pagans and others.

We'll be considering some historic interfaith encounters, plus reflecting on the experiences and writings of previous generations of Quakers as growing points and pointers for positive interfaith relations in future. We'll note, too, some

1

twentieth- and twenty-first century publications by Quakers both on particular religions and on interfaith understanding, and we will be sharing a few examples of contemporary interactions between Quakers and people of other faiths.

Just to be clear from the outset, in the following pages, 'other faiths' refers to non-Christian religions, not to any Christian churches or denominations. As we'll see, Quakers (especially 'liberal' Quakers) feel some strong affinities with certain aspects of other faiths while, at the same time, they may struggle with more traditionally Protestant and Catholic parts of the western Christian tradition. I realise that, despite Quakerism's Christian history, some Quakers today who do not self-define as Christian may well tend to regard Christianity as another faith. However, for the purposes of this publication, people of 'other faiths' are Baha'is, Buddhists, Hindus, Jains, Jews, Muslims, Sikhs, Pagans. They include Māori in New Zealand/Aotearoa as well as Australian Aboriginals and (with reference to the seventeenth century at least) Native Americans. 'Faith' encompasses far more than the so-called, and variously defined, 'world faiths'.

So humanists too are included. While not a religion in one usual (God-centred) sense of the word 'faith', humanism does (like conventional religions) offer a world-view and a moral framework and Humanists UK (formerly the British Humanist Association) contributes to discussion of the curricular subject of religious education in UK schools. Moreover, as a self-styled Quaker humanist, David Boulton has pointed out, humanists – and for that matter those who dedicate their lives to other -isms too – certainly live out faith in its core meaning of hope and trust.[1]

Following several theological splits that occurred in the nineteenth century, today's Quakers are themselves religiously diverse. In the USA, liberal 'Hicksite' Friends emphasised the guidance of the 'Inward Light'. 'Orthodox' Friends (just like the other Protestant churches) prioritised biblical authority over personal experience, and their missionaries evangelised in Africa and South America. Today, Quaker meetings in the USA are, variously, liberal, conservative, pastoral or evangelical, according to their belief about Christ and their style of worship.[2] As a result of missions by evangelical Friends, the majority of Quakers now live, not in the UK (where Quakerism began) nor in North America (which the first two Quakers reached in 1656), but in Africa. In fact, nearly half the global Quaker population lives in Kenya. These Quakers, like the Quakers of South America, are evangelical rather than liberal. The twentieth- and twenty-first-century publications mentioned in this booklet are, however, mainly by liberal Friends from Britain Yearly Meeting and Friends General Conference in the United States of America and Canada, even though liberal Friends comprise only some 11 per cent of Quakers worldwide.

These are the Friends who have unprogrammed, largely silent meetings for worship, and who employ no pastors. Their theology continues the emphases of the influential American Quaker, Rufus Jones (1863–1948), and his British contemporary, John Wilhelm Rowntree (1868–1905), on the 'inner light' and 'that of God in everyone'. Moreover, by contrast with the more exclusively and explicitly Christ-centred beliefs of evangelical Quakers, many liberal Quakers' spirituality nowadays consciously draws from multiple spiritual sources, rather than only Christian ones. Liberal Friends are travellers whose outlook is being changed by their journeying.

We will be following Quakers' interfaith journeying from the seventeenth and eighteenth centuries, during which even the names of days and months were rejected as too 'heathen' (as they perpetuated the names of pre-Christian deities such as Woden and Mars), to the present century in which boundaries between liberal Quakers and Pagans have sometimes blurred. The journey has included seeking to persuade others as well as considerable receptiveness to unfamiliar truths. It has been mapped, to a greater or lesser extent (and not always happily), by the principles expressed in the Quaker testimonies.

Throughout the centuries, Quakers have, nonetheless, realised the importance of good relationships with people of other faiths and they have usually shown great respect for their beliefs and practices. Quakers have published guidance on building interfaith relationships and given accounts of Quaker involvement in interfaith groups in North America and the UK. Do read them![3]

Chapter 2: Some early interfaith encounters

Long before any theological splits between evangelicals and liberals, Quakers had interacted with people of other faiths and – at least in the case of Quakerism's founder, George Fox (1624–1691) – they had engaged with other sacred writings. As early as 1673, Fox had addressed not only Christians but also 'the Jews and Turks throughout the World'. In other words, very unusually at that time, he did not exclude Muslims ('Turks') as enemies and irredeemable infidels. Fox, a Leicestershire weaver's son, wrote open letters to Muslims and Jews, encouraging them to accept Jesus as the only path to salvation. Even more remarkably, he quoted from the Qur'an when he wrote in 1680 to the king of Algiers about the plight of Quakers and other captives in his domain. (In fact, George Fox relied on a 1649 English translation, reputedly by King Charles I's chaplain, Alexander Ross, not of the original Qur'an but of a French translation.)

During the late 1670s, periodic reports of the extreme physical abuse, including sexual abuse, of Quaker and other captives in north Africa were reaching Quakers' executive body, Meeting for Sufferings (which had been established in 1675 to support Friends who were suffering persecution for their faith). Piracy was rife. Indeed, in 1671, on a voyage to Barbados, Fox himself had been travelling on a ship which narrowly escaped capture by north African pirates. In his letter, Fox tried to show the king that the ill treatment meted out to the captives fell far short of the ethical teachings in the Qur'an, which certainly condemned sexual abuse. Significantly, rather than denouncing Islam as a false religion, Fox's letter expressed more respect for the Qur'an than the translator, Ross, himself had done. What was more, Fox pointed out that Quaker captives could meet for worship in Morocco, while Quakers had less freedom to do so in England.

Even before Fox's addresses, Quaker missionaries had identified Muslims as potentially receptive to their message of God's indwelling Spirit (rather than regarding them as beyond the pale) and had tried to bring them to the truth out of concern for their spiritual welfare. It was with this intention that, in 1657, George Robinson had set out to the Middle East and reached Jerusalem, Gaza and Ramleh, a town at the intersection of the route between Cairo and Damascus and the road from Jaffa to Jerusalem. Although the Catholic friars were unfriendly, because George Robinson refused to visit the sacred sites (and so to pay them for the privilege of doing so), he was received in a friendly way by both 'Turks' and Jews.

The following year, a Yorkshire housemaid, Mary Fisher (c. 1623–1698), travelled to Turkey in order to share the truth of God's indwelling spirit with the 'Great Turk', the young sultan, Mohammed (or Mehmet) IV. Mary was one of the intrepid 'Valiant Sixty', the first-generation Quakers who travelled far and wide to preach as 'publishers of the truth'. In England the response could be hostile. Indeed, in 1652 she had been imprisoned for rebuking the vicar of Selby. In Cambridge, soon after this, her efforts to re-educate the theological students of Sidney Sussex College had resulted in her being publicly flogged. Nor had she met with milder treatment overseas. In 1656, in Boston (where she was one of the first two Quakers to set foot in America), the local Puritans' anger at her preaching had led to her being publicly stripped so as to search her for any physical signs that she was a witch. She was then imprisoned with the intention (which was mercifully thwarted by a local sympathiser) of starving her to death.

By contrast with this violent response from her fellow Christians, Mary Fisher was received respectfully in the sultan's court. Thanks to the three attendant interpreters, she communicated her message to him and 'the sultan was very noble unto me and understood every word I said'. On her return to England, she reported: 'They are more near Truth than many nations; there is a love begot in me towards them which is endless...'[4]

A Canadian researcher, David Vlasblom, has reflected, 'The Quakers were much better suited than their fellow early modern English and Western European Christian religionists to learn lessons from other cultures because their religion did not prejudice them against Muslims and other cultures but rather encouraged dialogue.'[5] Nor did Quakers respond to violence with violence. Thus, in 1663, when Turks captured his ship, Thomas Lurting succeeded in disarming them while they were asleep, and then treated them well, so escaping slavery for himself and the crew.

While seafaring Quakers were interacting with Muslims, George Fox's wife, Margaret Fell, wrote four epistles to the Jews, whom she regarded as being as open as anyone else to the Inward Light which enables all to become like Christ. Fell drew on her reading of the Hebrew literature that comprised the Christians' Old Testament and she had her own epistles translated into Hebrew. In 1655, Oliver Cromwell allowed the return of Jews to England (from which they had been expelled in 1290) and Margaret Fell saw this as an opportunity for Jews to encounter and adopt true (Protestant) Christian religion in the sense of turning to their 'Inward Teacher (the Torah of the Heart)', which would be a necessary precursor to Christ's second coming. From a Jewish perspective, of course, this seems an unsatisfactorily conditional welcome.

As regards George Fox's views, a nineteenth-century writer, Samuel Janney, reported him as saying 'the Jews who had the Scriptures, did not understand them, because they resisted the Holy Spirit'.[6] It is interesting and a little disheartening, too, to note the disenfranchisement of Jews in the Quaker colony of Pennsylvania which William Penn (1644–1718) founded in 1681. On the one hand, his colony attracted Jews, like other persecuted groups – Quakers, other Protestants, and Catholics – and in Pennsylvania Jews were, like them, free to worship, but they were, unlike them, (as was the case for Jews in Britain too) debarred from voting.

In London, a few years later, a Quaker carpenter, Joseph Avis, is remembered positively by Jews for designing Kahal Kadosh Shaar Asamaim (Holy Congregation the Gates of Heaven) better known as the Bevis Marks synagogue in Aldgate, in the City of London. The synagogue dates from 1701, when Spanish and Portuguese Jews were fleeing the Inquisition, and it is Britain's oldest functioning synagogue. Joseph Avis had worked with the famous architect Christopher Wren and he reputedly returned to the Jewish congregation the difference between his original higher estimate and the final cost.

As well as individual English Quakers' interactions with Jews and Muslims, seventeenth-century Quakers in North America encountered Native Americans and their spirituality. In 1682, William Penn, the Quaker founder of the state of Pennsylvania, 'spoke to Native Americans, as an equal in their own language' (which he had made an effort to learn) of 'the Great Spirit who made me and you'.[7] Penn's words, published in 1693, appear in successive Quaker 'books of discipline' (see below). He wrote:

> The humble, meek, merciful, just, pious, and devout souls are everywhere of one religion: and when death has taken off the mask they will know one another, though the divers liveries they wear here makes them strangers.[8]

Interestingly, Penn likened the Native Americans to Jews:

> For their original, I am ready to believe them of the Jewish race, I mean of the stock of the ten tribes, and that for the following reasons: first, they were to go to a land not planted nor known, which to be sure Asia and Africa were, if not

8

Europe; and He who intended that extraordinary judgement upon them might make the passage not uneasy to them, as it is not impossible in itself, from the easternmost parts of Asia to the westernmost of America. In the next place, I find them of the like countenance, and their children of so lively resemblance, that a man would think himself in Duke's Place or Berry Street in London, when he seeth them. But this is not all: they agree in rites; they reckon by moons; they offer their first fruits; they have a kind of feast of tabernacles; they are said to lay their altar upon twelve stones; their mourning a year; customs of women; with many other things that do not now occur.[9]

Penn noted, moreover, that the Indians' 'language is lofty, yet narrow, but, like the Hebrew in signification, full'.[10]

This comparison is from Penn's letter to the Free Society of Traders, following his visit to the interior of Pennsylvania in 1683, as reproduced in Samuel Janney's *Life of William Penn*. Penn described the indigenous people's language, houses, customs and diet, parenting and remedies, as well as their governance. He stressed their generosity and readiness to share, their contentment with very little, and the damaging effects on them of the liquor that the Europeans had brought. Regarding their 'religion' he observed:

These poor people are under a dark night in things relating to religion, to be sure the tradition of it: yet they say there is a great King, that made them, who dwells in a glorious country to the southward of them; and that the souls of the good shall go thither, where they shall live again. Their worship consists of two parts, sacrifice and cantico. Their sacrifice is their first fruits. The first and fattest buck they kill goeth to the fire, where he is all burnt, with a mournful ditty of him who performeth the ceremony, but with such marvellous fervency and labour of body, that he will even sweat to a foam.[11]

Penn continued:

> The other part is their cantico, performed by round dances, sometimes words, sometimes songs, then shouts; two being in the middle who begin, and by singing and drumming on a board, direct the chorus. Their postures in the dance are very antic and differing, but all keep measure. This is done with equal earnestness and labour, but great appearance of joy. In the fall, when the corn cometh in, they begin to feast one another. There have been two great festivals already, to which come all that will. I was at one myself.[12]

Subsequently, in North America, the noted Quaker preacher John Woolman (1720–1772), whose respect for other human beings and for animals meant he was both a staunch abolitionist and a vegetarian, reacted in a very positive way to 'heathen' Native Americans. So much so that, in 1762, he wrote:

> There is a principle, which is pure, placed in the human mind, which in different places and ages hath different names: it is, however, pure and proceeds from God. It is deep and inward, confined to no forms of religion nor excluded from any where the heart stands in perfect sincerity. In whomsoever this takes root and grows, of what nation soever, they become brethren.[13]

Similarly, Robert Barclay (1648–1690), the seventeenth-century Scottish Quaker theologian, had contended that the 'light of Christ' enabled anyone – including non-Christians – to find truth and serve God. In early editions of his *Apology*, Barclay referred to Hayy Ibn Yaqzan, a character in an allegorical novel by the twelfth-century Muslim philosopher Abu Bakr Ibn Tufayl. Hayy Ibn Yaqzan's knowledge of God and communion with God had developed in complete isolation from any other human being. However, although in Barclay's view Christians could learn from non-Christian teachings, he condemned 'Mahomet' as an 'Impostor' even so and denounced the two 'false opinions' held by Muslims, namely that it was 'unlawful' to drink wine and that it was lawful to 'keep many concubines'.[14] Nonetheless, in 1678 Robert Barclay made possibly his best-known – and unambiguously inclusive – statement and this has appeared in successive books of Quaker discipline:

> There may be members therefore of this Catholic [i.e., universal Christian] church both among heathens, Turks, Jews, and all the several sorts of Christians, men and women of integrity and simplicity of heart, who... are by the secret touches of this holy light in their souls, enlivened and quickened, thereby secretly united to God, and there-through become true members of this Catholic church.[15]

Of course, Barclay's inclusivity in no way departs from or challenges an unquestioningly Christian worldview. Interestingly, his insight foreshadows the idea of 'anonymous Christians', which was articulated by the twentieth-century German Jesuit priest and theologian Karl Rahner (1904–1984). In Rahner's view God's grace is present in all times and all places and even those who have never heard the gospel are saved by Christ if (without realising that they are in fact responding to God's grace as manifest in Jesus's life) they love their neighbours, are prepared for death and adopt an attitude of hope for the future. Understandably, not every adherent of another faith would comfortably accept the (well-meaning) judgement either that they are 'true members of this Catholic church' or that they are 'anonymous Christians'.

From the seventeenth century onward, members of other faith communities were forming their own views of the Quakers whom they met. In the mid-1680s, Quakers' 'Meeting for Sufferings' in London heard from a former captive, Ephraim Gilbert, that 'The Turks and Moors say that the Q[uake]rs are a simple Innocent people, they know they won't steal'.[16]

Naturally, most Quakers have not been theologians or philosophers. Moreover, not all the Quakers who have met with people of other faiths have adhered to Quaker principles or even been 'simple innocent people'. One less than exemplary Quaker was the multilingual nineteenth-century American adventurer, soldier and self-educated physician Josiah Harlan (1799–1871) who rejoiced in the title 'Prince of Ghor'. Harlan had dealings with Buddhists, Hindus, Sikhs and Muslims, as he served in Burma and Bengal and Punjab as well as being almost certainly the first American to set foot in Afghanistan. In Punjab he met with the Sikh maharaja, Ranjit Singh, and enraged him by demanding an exorbitant advance payment for medical treatment. In consequence, Harlan transferred his services to Afghanistan's Muslim ruler, Dost Mohammed, whom he encouraged to declare war on Ranjit Singh. Interestingly, when Harlan eventually returned to America, he was reaccepted into Quaker membership after having been disowned for not being a pacifist. He had not only fought but had also raised an army.

Chapter 3: Interfaith pointers in Quakers' books of discipline

Local Quaker meetings belong to Yearly Meetings (which, of course, meet annually). Britain has a single Yearly Meeting, formerly known as London Yearly Meeting and now as Britain Yearly Meeting. There are, however, many more Yearly Meetings in the United States, providing for the spectrum of belief and styles of worship previously mentioned. Several Yearly Meetings publish a periodically updated 'book of discipline' which sets out what being a Quaker entails. During Meeting for Worship, a copy of the Yearly Meeting's book of discipline is placed alongside the Bible on the table and passages are frequently read and pondered during worship.

In London Yearly Meeting, from 1921, the compilers' method was, increasingly, to convey what being a Quaker involves by reproducing Quakers' own articulations of their experience, rather than through more formal statements of belief and practice. In line with this approach, in 1960 London Yearly Meeting published *Christian Faith and Practice in the Experience of the Society of Friends*. In German translation it is also used by Friends in Germany and Austria.

Of the 677 extracts, five (interestingly in a section headed 'Friends and the Christian Church') directly concerned 'Friends and other faiths'.

Moreover, the much longer section entitled 'Spiritual experiences of Friends' quotes Inazo Nitoe (1862–1933) an agricultural reformer, scholar and prolific writer, and Under-Secretary-general of the League of Nations in Geneva. By birth Nitoe was a member of Japan's ancient military caste, the samurai, with a heritage of Buddhist, Zen, Confucian and Shinto insights. In his 1927 publication 'A Japanese View of Quakerism', he had written:

13

Only in Quakerism could I reconcile Christianity with Oriental thought. Let it be far from me to turn Quakerism into Oriental mysticism. Quakerism stays within the family of Christianity. It professes to rest its structure on the person of Jesus Christ, whom it identifies with the Inner Light... it believes His grace was retro-active, so that it was He who enlightened all the seers of old.... Curiously enough, the Cosmic sense, as described by those who attain it, is very much the same everywhere – whether it be a Buddhist priest, a Shinto votary, a Mohammedan saint, a French mathematician, an American farmer, or a Jewish philosopher.[17]

As is the tradition in the Society, the content of *Christian Faith and Practice* was, a generation later, carefully and prayerfully revised, in accordance with Quaker procedure for practical decision-making. *Quaker Faith and Practice* duly appeared in 1995. Section 9. 21 summarises Friends and interfaith relations and, in section 27, headed 'Unity and diversity', not five but eleven excerpts from Friends' writings relate to 'Friends and other faiths'.

Both volumes reproduced the passages (partially quoted above) by William Penn ('The humble, meek, merciful, just, pious, and devout souls are everywhere of one religion...') and by Robert Barclay, and they both also reproduced the words of Marjorie Sykes, a Quaker educationist who devoted her life to wide-ranging service in India. In *Quaker Signposts*, Stephanie Ramamurthy, another British Quaker with strong links to India, likens Sykes to John Woolman in her principled and prescient dedication to simplicity, peace-making and environmental sustainability.[18] Marjorie Sykes's quotation concludes:

We all know the fruits of the Spirit, and recognise the beauty of holiness, in our own ancestral tree... The flowers of unselfish living may be found growing in other men's gardens and... rich fruits of the Spirit may be tasted from other men's trees.

14

They spring from the same Holy Spirit of Truth, the same seed of God, whose power moves us through Christ.[19]

She would have expected readers to recognise her invocation of St Paul's letter to the people of Galatia (central Anatolia) in the New Testament, in which he wrote: 'But the fruit of the Spirit is love, joy, peace, longsuffering, kindness, goodness, faithfulness'.[20]

Christian Faith and Practice also included words from the Quaker historian Margaret Hobling's Swarthmore lecture of 1958, a year after the publication of Marjorie Sykes's words. The Swarthmore Lecture is an annual lecture with the purpose of interpreting to the members of the Society of Friends their message and mission and bringing to public notice the spirit, aims and fundamental principles of Friends. In the book associated with her lecture, Hobling observed that 'an increasing number of people have had personal contacts with humble men and holy of heart in all walks of life of whom they dare not deny that they have been taught of God'.[21] Clearly, for Britain's Quakers, as for members of other Christian denominations, a major impetus to approaching other faiths with respect has been the imperative of being a good neighbour to newcomers from different faith backgrounds and, coupled with this, a recognition of their new neighbours' attributes – their hospitality, courage and industriousness.

British society was to change further in the period between the publication of *Christian Faith and Practice* in 1960 and *Quaker Faith and Practice* in 1995, with far more people in the UK having contact with people of other faiths. Laws on immigration and race relations were the British government's response to the increasing diversity of many cities. The content of Quakers' books of discipline provides another small pointer to the social change that was underway.

In this increasingly multifaith Britain the compilers of *Quaker Faith and Practice* included not only more recent reflections but also John Woolman's words from 1763:

15

Love was the first motion, and then a concern arose to spend some time with the Indians, that I might feel and understand their life, and the Spirit they live in, if haply I might receive some instruction from them, or they be in any degree helped forward by my following the leadings of Truth amongst them.[22]

Among the additional excerpts were words written by Henry T. Hodgkin in 1933. He had played a leading part in the Friends Foreign Mission Association, and he had worked as a missionary in China. In the process Hodgkin had come to 'appreciate the validity of other witnesses to God than the Christian one', as the introductory rubric in *Quaker Faith and Practice* explains. To quote from Hodgkin:

I recognise [a change] to have taken place in myself, from a certain assumption that mine was really the better way, to a very complete recognition that there is no one better way, and that God needs all kinds of people and ways of living through which to manifest himself in the world.[23]

Other passages too from *Quaker Faith and Practice* indicate a growing discomfort among British Friends with the limitations of the label 'Christian', together with a growing readiness to learn from others. This shift is evident in the distilled guidance in the 42 'Advices and Queries' with which *Quaker Faith and Practice* starts – Advices and Queries that are used not only in Britain but by Quakers in Australia and (in Danish translation) in Denmark. As explained under the heading 'Duty of Reading':

Advices and queries are intended for use in Quaker meetings, for private devotion and reflection, as a challenge and inspiration to us as Friends in our personal lives and in our life as a religious community, and as a concise expression of our faith and practice for enquirers and the wider world.[24]

Accordingly, *Advices and Queries* (1995) offers direction for relating to 'other communities of faith':

Do you work gladly with other religious groups in the pursuit of common goals? While remaining faithful to Quaker insights, try to enter imaginatively into the life and witness of other communities of faith creating together the bonds of friendship. Be aware of the Spirit of God at work in the ordinary activities and experience of your daily life. Spiritual learning continues throughout life, and often in unexpected ways. There is inspiration to be found in all around us... Are you open to new light, from whatever source it may come? Do you approach new ideas with discernment?[25]

The previous (1964) *Advices and Queries* had already asked:

Are you loyal to the Truth, and do you keep your mind open to new light, from whatever it may arise? Are you giving time and thought to the study of the Bible, and other writings which reveal the ways of God? Do you recognise the spiritual contribution made by other faiths?[26]

Bearing in mind this encouragement to 'work gladly with other religious groups in the pursuit of common goals', to read widely and to be 'open to new light', as well as Quakers' testimony to justice and equality, Australian Friends' book of discipline has a section on 'Indigenous people' (see chapter 12) and *Quaker Faith and Practice Aotearoa/New Zealand* includes interactions with Māori. We now turn, however, to Quakers' engagement in the twentieth and twenty-first centuries with Muslims and Jews.

Chapter 4: Muslims

Britain Yearly Meeting's 1995 book of discipline, *Quaker Faith and Practice*, includes the Quaker writer John Punshon's experience at an interfaith gathering in his home city of Birmingham:

> The discussion was about prayer and I confessed that it was my habit to pray anywhere and that I could do so sitting comfortably in a chair. A devout Muslim woman in the conference was shocked at what she saw as my easygoing familiarity with God, my lack of respect, my denial of my own human dignity. When you think of God, she said, there is only one possible response. It is to go down on your *knees*.
>
> From this unnamed woman I learned something of Islam – submission to God – in a way that no Christian had ever taught me... It was not the Mosque or the Qur'an addressing me, but the living God I know in Christ speaking through her.[27]

Certainly, Punshon's reflection illustrates openness to new light.

Unsurprisingly, whether they have met Muslims or not, many Quakers find inspiration in translations of the thirteenth-century Sufi poet Jalal Ad-Din Muhammad Rumi, better known simply as Rumi. As the 'progressive Christian Quaker theologian' Daniel P. Coleman suggests, it is easy to detect parallels between Sufis and Quakers as a mystical element in Islam and Christianity respectively.[28] Moreover, as another Friend, the American interfaith practitioner Anthony Manousos, has pointed out, both Sufis and Quakers value simplicity and silence. (Sufis take their name from the simple woollen clothing that they used to wear.) An inner simplicity characterises both Sufi and Quaker worship, and both Sufis and Quakers may fill their silence with recollected – and sometimes wordless – prayer. Manousos quotes the fourteenth-century Baha-ad-din Naqshband, the founder of Sufis' Naqshbandi Order, declaring, 'God is silence, and is most easily reached in silence.'[29]

At the same time, it needs to be remembered that, while Sufi shrines and saints bring spiritual solace to countless Muslims, for many other Muslims Sufism and Rumi himself are unacceptable. Clearly, from the perspective of Islamic State, to take the most extreme example, Sufism is idolatrous and its popularity threatens their own hold on the Muslim masses. Hence the brutal attacks this century on Sufi shrines in Syria, Pakistan, Egypt, Libya, Mali and elsewhere.

Horrifying as these attacks have been, it is the 9/11 attack by al-Qaeda on the World Trade Center in New York in 2001 that has shaken the world most profoundly. Along with many other concerned citizens, Quakers – in the US especially – responded by seeking out local mosques, expressing solidarity with local Muslims and reading translations of the Qur'an and the writings of Muslims and others about Islam. Quakers invited Muslims to speak in their meetings and also examined in depth their own level of understanding of Islam and of Muslims' experience. Anthony Manousos, described how he felt impelled to keep the fast of Ramadan from 17 November 2001 and to incorporate Muslim prayers in his own daily practice. On realising that Manousos, a non-Muslim, was maintaining the fast, Muslims began questioning him about Quakerism.[30]

For some late twentieth- and early twenty-first-century Friends in the UK and in North America the experience of learning from Islam, and from Sufi Islam especially, has led them to become Muslims themselves. An increasing (though small) number of Quakers have adopted Islam without feeling either that their Quaker loyalty is compromised or that they cannot fully embrace Islam. To take two examples, Brett Miller-White and Christopher Bagley are Muslim Quakers. In his article on 'the making of a Muslim Quaker' Miller-White wrote of Muslims' respect for Jesus as a prophet and teacher rather than as God and he mentioned too the appeal of Sufi tradition. He found his own multiple identity unproblematic and spoke of 'my hybrid culture'.[31] Christopher Bagley (a Jew by birth who first adopted Christianity, then Quakerism and, finally, Islam) wrote 'Islam Today: A Muslim Quaker's View' which appeared as a Quaker Universalist Group pamphlet.[32]

At the same time that individual Quakers have adopted Islam, a few Muslims have engaged with Quakers. Another Quaker Quicks author, the British Quaker John Lampen, reported: 'Two Bosnian Muslims who attended my local meeting for worship said afterwards, "You say God and we say Allah, but at the level of spirit we are one."'[33]

One Muslim who has entered deeply into Quakerism is Naveed Moheen. He speaks of practising Islam in a Quakerly manner. To quote Moheen:

> There is a verse in the *Qur'an* that goes *Qul kulluny ya'malu 'alaa shaakilatihee fa rabbukum a'lamu biman huwa ahdaa sabeelaa*, which translates loosely as 'Let everyone act according to their own disposition. It is only God who knows who is truly on the right path.'
>
> And to me, that embraces both Islam and how Friends think about coming to the Light. As Friends, we know that there are multiple, legitimate ways to the Light, and personally I don't see a conflict between that and what Islam teaches.[34]

Moheen found a resonance between Quakers' sense of a 'gathered meeting' and the Islamic principle of *jamia*, a gathering with a spiritual purpose. Moreover, he likened Quakers' belief in 'the messages that come from the divine' with the Qur'an coming as a message through Mohammed. He ended his testimony by stating that, with regard to Islam and Quakerism:

I found that—and I still find—that there is no difference in the fundamental principles of loving your fellow human being, of being able to walk in the Light with others and of seeking the good in others.[35]

Similarly, Anthony Manousos has shared the parallels between Islam in general and the Quaker testimonies. As well as the shared emphasis on community, there is simplicity – evident in the plainness of both meeting houses and mosques – plus there is the emphasis on Islam as a religion of peace (although violence is allowed in some circumstances). The Qur'an enjoins Muslims: 'Repel evil with what is better, then will the one with whom there is enmity become an intimate friend.'[36] Moreover, the principles of equality and of integrity are affirmed by both Muslims and Quakers. Also, as Manousos points out, many liberal Friends' respect for Jesus' teachings (such as 'Love your enemies') coupled with their unreadiness to worship him as divine, is closer to Muslims' stance than to that of traditional Christians, including Christ-centred Friends.[37]

In the seventeenth century parallels had sometimes been drawn between Muslims and Quakers by those who wished to malign both communities. However, when George Fox, George Robinson and Mary Fisher attempted to share their truth with 'Turks' they probably never imagined a time when some individuals could identify themselves as Quaker Muslims or Muslim Quakers.

As a footnote, with regard to the Quaker-Muslim interface in the early twentieth and twenty-first centuries, the Quaker chocolate manufacturer and philanthropist Edward Cadbury merits a mention. In the 1920s Cadbury financed three journeys to the Middle East, by a Chaldean collector, Alphonse Mingana, to collect manuscripts for Woodbrooke, the Quaker college in Birmingham. The manuscripts included what turned out (thanks to radiocarbon dating nearly a century later) to be one of the oldest surviving fragments of the Qur'an – parts of surahs 18 to 20, written in Hijazi, an early Arabic script, on parchment dating from during, or shortly after, the prophet Muhammad's lifetime.

As we will see, the Middle East (or west Asia, from another, non-European perspective) has been a significant factor in more recent Quaker relations with both Muslims and Jews.

Chapter 5: Jews

Out of all Quakers' relationships with other communities of faith, the closest, most complex and at times most painful has been with Jews, as traced by the Jewish Quaker writer Tony Stoller in his article titled 'The End of the Affair?'[38] Jews are the faith community most akin to Christianity, and – especially in earlier centuries – Quakers grew up steeped in the Hebrew scriptures that constitute Christians' Old Testament.

They also shared with other Christians a certainty that Christians now replaced Jews as God's chosen people. These traditionally 'supersessionist' tendencies have implications for relations between Quakers and Jews, as Stuart Masters, who is programme coordinator for history and theology at Woodbrooke Quaker Study Centre, has explored.[39]

The relationship that began, as we have seen, with George Fox and his wife, Margaret Fell, has been shaped during the past hundred years by Quaker response, firstly, to the tragedies of Hitler's genocide in Europe and, subsequently, to Palestinians' suffering in the state of Israel. While Quakers' compassion and their faithfulness to their testimony of justice were a constant in both contexts, some Jews have come to regard Quakers (and some other Christian groups) as fickle and no longer sympathetic and supportive but quite the reverse.

This down-turn needs to be seen in the context of twentieth-century relations from earlier in the century: in 1917 Rufus Jones co-founded the American Friends Service Committee (AFSC), which played a key role in helping refugees, including many Jews, to escape Nazi Germany in the 1930s. After Kristallnacht (the night of 9–10 November 1938, when a Nazi-masterminded pogrom was unleashed against Jews throughout Germany), Jones pleaded with Reinhard Heydrich, one of the principal architects of the Holocaust, for better treatment of Jews. The AFSC supported not only observant Jews but also the non-religious Jews and the Jews who had married non-Jews, and it was pivotal in organising the kindertransport which transferred 12,000 Jewish children to safety in Britain.

Quakers in Britain welcomed these young refugees and Quaker schools waived their fees. Among many other British Quakers, Eleanor Rathbone (1872–1946), a tireless humanitarian activist and MP, is remembered for her efforts to rescue refugees. Israel's World Holocaust Remembrance Center recognised as 'Righteous Among the Nations' thirteen Quakers who had helped to save Jews and the US Holocaust Memorial Museum in Washington D.C. similarly acknowledges the AFSC for 'helping people flee Nazi Europe, communicate with loved ones, and adjust to life in the US'.

The fact that some Jews have attended Quaker meetings and, indeed, have become members of the Religious Society of Friends, is largely due to this crucial intervention and support. Also, unlike (other) Christian churches, Quakers require neither baptism nor affirmations of belief, both of which could be problematic to seekers from Jewish and other faith backgrounds. The Jewish Quaker writer Harvey Gillman has acknowledged the 'universalist resonances' between their faiths as the 'Quaker desire to see the divine in all people is attractive to many Jews'.[40] Another Jewish Quaker writer, Margot Tennyson, who had personal experience of a Liberal synagogue, explained, 'I became a Friend because I was drawn to the Silence, and found in it the possibility to grow in my spiritual understanding.'[41] Similarly, in 2016 Sue Beardon wrote of 'the waiting silence' that she experienced in Quaker meetings.[42] She identified a shared 'radical vison of a better world that we as human beings, with the guidance and collaboration of the Spirit, can achieve here on earth' and the fact that neither Quakers nor Jews feel a 'need for a temple'. Perhaps other Jewish Quakers would echo her disclosure that 'Quakerism is something I chose. Jewishness I can never shake off'.[43]

Without becoming Quakers themselves, many twentieth-century Jews felt a deep affinity with Quakers. The well-known

BBC radio 4 personality Rabbi Lionel Blue acknowledged how it was at a Quaker meeting that he found a resolution to severe personal conflicts. 'I literally fell among Quakers when I went up to Oxford.'[44]

Nonetheless, the present century has seen tensions rise because of Quakers' concerns over the Israeli state's treatment of Palestinians. At first sight, both the Quaker testimonies to justice and peace are a natural fit with harmonious interfaith relationships. The complex history of Quaker-Jewish relations, however, illustrates the fact that the concerns and actions of Quakers and others, whose motivation is to expose and ease the oppression of Palestinians, are viewed as politically partisan by the Israeli government and its supporters, most of whom are Jewish.

In 2015 the Quaker Committee for Christian and Interfaith Relations (QCCIR) stated: 'The Jewish-Quaker dialogue is highly sensitive in the light of both our historical support and BYM's [Britain Yearly Meeting's] current ethical political stance on the Occupied Territories.'[45] Here, 'Occupied Territories' referred to the Gaza Strip and the West Bank (including East Jerusalem), part of the former British Mandate for Palestine, which have been militarily occupied by Israel ever since the Six-Day War of 1967.

Of particular concern to pro-Israeli Jews has been the activity of WCC-EAPPI, the World Council of Churches' Ecumenical Accompaniment Programme in Palestine and Israel. EAPPI's advocacy 'for justice and peace based on non-violence and a non-partisan approach' chime with core Quaker values and, in the UK and Ireland, EAPPI is in fact administered by Quakers in Britain on behalf of 16 partner churches and NGOs. Since its creation in 2002, EAPPI has provided a continuous input of 25 to 30 Ecumenical Accompaniers. They serve for three months at a time in accompanying, offering a protective presence, and witness at, for example, Israeli check-points or during the demolition of Palestinians' properties.

Despite its stated non-partisan intent, EAPPI's programme is viewed by many Jews as hostile to the Jewish state. Some returning Accompaniers, they allege, have voiced anti-Semitic views when addressing meetings. Many Jews' negative view of Quakers had reached a climax following the decision by Meeting for Sufferings in London in 2011 to boycott goods from Israeli settlements in Judea and Samaria. 'How Quakers Turned Spiteful' is the title of an article in the *Jewish Chronicle* of 27 April 2011. Quakers are, the writer claimed, preoccupied with alleviating suffering but not sympathetic to the concept of Jewish self-determination. Indeed, the writer suggested, the 'political objectives' of Meeting for Sufferings (the executive body of Quakers in Britain) are 'to demonise the Jewish state and to ethnically cleanse Jews from the West Bank and the Holy City'. In his view, 'Jewish rights and Jewish suffering are – ultimately – of marginal importance to the world order as Quakers envisage it.'[46] He informed his readers that '[t]he resolution waxed lyrical on the work of "Jewish Israeli Peace Groups" and the need to support their partisan efforts'. Admittedly, in 1948, he conceded: 'the Quakers did indeed send missions to both Israel and Gaza' but, he pointed out, 'their ultimate aim was to repatriate Arab "refugees" and thus to undermine the establishment of a Jewish state.'[47]

In the *Wall Street Journal* and in *Tablet* (a Jewish magazine), articles by Alexander Joffe and Asaf Romirowsky include equally strongly-worded accusations, claiming that Quakers' 'benign reputation masks a tough campaign to boycott the Jewish state' and that the AFSC 'has gone from saving Jews to vilifying them'.[48]

However, by no means all Joffe's and Romirowsky's co-religionists denounce Quakers in this way. When Israel included the AFSC on its 2018 blacklist of 20 social justice groups it would ban for supporting the Boycott, Divestment and Sanctions movement, Brant Rosen expressed dismay at the 'hypocrisy of those who applaud the Quakers' work on behalf of Jewish refugees, yet bitterly criticize them for applying the very same values and efforts on behalf of Palestinian refugees'.[49] Rosen was a rabbi working for AFSC and he had co-founded the Jewish Voice for Peace Rabbinical Council. Likewise, *Haaretz* (a liberal Israeli newspaper founded a century earlier in 1918) proclaimed that 'Israel's blacklisting of Quakers is a crime against Jewish History' and 'It is another example of how often those who claim to speak on behalf of Jewish dignity and power often turn out to be the cowards that debase Jewish history most of all'.[50]

Naturally, this unresolved and acrimonious state of affairs is harrowing for Jewish Quakers and, indeed, more widely the many Jews with Quaker connections and Quakers with Jewish connections. Already, following Yearly Meeting in Bath, UK, in 2014 a Quaker group had formed with the name 'Friends with Jewish Connections' which 'provides support to Quaker members and attenders who have Jewish connections, as they discern how they can best help Quaker-Jewish dialogue'. As Harvey Gillman wrote in his article about the group in 2017:

> We are very aware of the bitterness felt on all sides. We do not have simple answers. Some of us are conflicted internally. Indeed, several of us have shared how we ourselves have been the victims of anti-Semitism on the one hand and yet are called self-hating on the other, if as Jews we are critical of the policies of the state of Israel.[51]

Because of the inseparability of religious identity from some national politics and intercommunal conflict, Quaker challenges to perceived injustices can make relations with some faith communities more precarious. Indeed, *Quakers and Other Faiths*, a document that was published by QCCIR for the use of Quaker institutions and local Quaker meetings, poses the question: 'Where do we make a stand recognising that some issues cannot be bypassed in the interests of good will?'[52]

Chapter 6: Quaker interfaith approaches

Arguably the single strongest momentum towards increasing inter-faith understanding in the west in the nineteenth century came from the 1893 Parliament of Religions in Chicago, addressed by – among others – the remarkable Hindu apologist Swami Vivekananda. Two Quakers attended, one Hicksite (liberal) and the other orthodox and evangelical.

In exploring published Quaker approaches to other faiths and to interfaith relations in the twentieth and twenty-first centuries, it is instructive to note the development in parallel of a theology of faiths among Roman Catholics, Anglicans, Methodists and other Christian denominations. However, with their creedal statements, their doctrinal emphasis on the uniqueness of Christ and on the need for salvation (which is only available through Christ), and with their history of evangelism, these churches faced deeper challenges than liberal Quakers have done in accommodating non-Christian religions in their theological understanding. Broadly, in the analysis by Anglican theologian Alan Race and others, in the latter decades of the twentieth century three approaches to other faiths are evident in Christian theological discourse, namely exclusivism, inclusivism and pluralism.[53] Theologians' discussions of these three positions – in many cases asserting their inadequacy and lack of nuance – have generated a substantial corpus of literature. The one-sentence encapsulations that follow are simply the most basic of signage of the terrain for readers who are unfamiliar with it. Exclusivism, as the name suggests, is the view that, among the world's faiths, only Christianity holds the ultimate truth and offers salvation. Inclusivism suggests that other religions too can in fact be vehicles of Christian salvation for their adherents. Pluralism accepts that different religions have their own validity. The philosopher of religions John Hick (who was to become a Quaker in later life) pictured the religions in orbit around the one ultimate reality which he termed 'the Real', and he shared his conviction that the spiritual and moral fruits evident in the lives of people of all faiths make any exclusive claims for the superiority of any one faith untenable.[54]

If such labels are to be applied to liberal Quaker thinking on the relationship between faiths, pluralist provides the closest match, and Robert Barclay's approach was inclusivist. However, what Quakers have prioritised is not theorising about how Christianity can accommodate the existence of other religions but rather how Quakers best relate to people from different faith communities and cultural backgrounds. Arising from their respect for the indwelling spirit, the inner light or 'that of God in everyone', a discerning openness, rather than reservations based on dogma, tends to characterise Quakers' attitude.

In the case of successive twentieth-century Quaker thinkers about interfaith relations, it was their personal involvement in India and other Asian countries, rather than any engagement with developments in more mainstream Christian theology, that was catalytic. Furthermore, following the Second World War, a wave of fascination with eastern religions swept across western countries and deepened the interest of Friends no less than other seekers, and this continues to be the case. A British Quaker, Damaris Parker-Rhodes, conveyed this in her 1977 Swarthmore lecture:

A number of Friends both here and in America, are at the present time in this movement of search, practising Transcendental Meditation [TM], learning Yoga and T'ai Chi, Zen and Theravada meditation and working with Sufis – and I count myself among them. This is not just shopping around, but is rather a serious experiment with truth which for me has made Quaker Christianity the more precious.[55]

What others might dismiss as syncretism was in fact a considered commitment to testing and experiencing (profoundly and ecstatically in the case of Parker-Rhodes and Sufism) from a widening spiritual repertoire while, at the same time, holding fast to Quaker principles.

Well before World War 2, consistently with earlier Quaker approaches to other faiths, the influential American Quaker writer Rufus Jones (1863–1948), had emphasised the concept of 'inner light' as intrinsic to the human condition whatever one's religious beliefs. In 1927 Jones visited India, met Mohandas Gandhi and went to Bodh Gaya, where Gautama Buddha had received enlightenment. Then he toured China. At the World Missionary Conference in Jerusalem, Jones urged the participants to be open to the positive influences from other world religions, 'gladly recognizing the good they contain'.[56]

What was more, Henry T. Hodgkin (1877–1930) arrived at this same conclusion, as we have seen in the quotation above from *Quaker Faith and Practice*. Hodgkin was not only the secretary of the Friends Foreign Mission Association, but he had also played a leading part in the Student Christian Movement and in founding the Christian pacifist organisation, the Fellowship of Reconciliation. On the subject of a Quaker attitude to foreign missions, Hodgkin declared that his new position regarding other faiths

has seemed to carry with it two conclusions which greatly affect conduct. One is that I really find myself wanting to learn from people whom I previously would have regarded as fit objects for my 'missionary zeal'. To discover another way in which God is operating – along lines it may be distasteful or dangerous to me – is a large part of the fun of living. The second direction in which conduct is influenced is the deliberate attempt to share the life and interests of others who are not in my circle … [for] in such sharing I can most deeply understand the other's life and through that reach, maybe, fresh truths about God.[57]

Seeking to understand Hindu spirituality better, Geoffrey Maw, a Quaker missionary, accompanied Hindu pilgrims in 1923, 1930 and 1934 on their journeys into the Himalaya mountains to the sources of the Ganga and recorded his efforts in his journal, which was published as *Pilgrims in Hindu Holy Land*.[58] In 1949 the Fellowship of the Friends of Truth was launched in Rasulia (in Hoshangabad, India) thanks to the initiative of another Quaker, Horace Alexander, who was working with Gandhi. As Margot Tennyson reported, the Fellowship aimed to encourage members of different faiths to worship together, and to support each other's efforts for world peace and social justice, while remaining true to their own faith. The Fellowship's basis was reverence for all religions, silent worship, and united action on nonviolent lines.[59]

Douglas Steere (1901–1995), an American Quaker ecumenist, whose career included organising post-war relief work in Finland, Norway and Poland, as well as his professorships in theology and philosophy, in 1971 published a pamphlet on 'mutual irradiation'. This insight arose from his experiences of opening himself to Hindu tradition in India and to Zen Buddhism in Japan. In his words: 'Something happens in the course of understanding another's truth that irradiates and lights up one's own tradition and that on rare occasions may even give one a hint of a truth that embraces both, a hidden convergence.'[60]

Another initiative as well owed much to the experience in India of a British Quaker, John Linton. He drew inspiration too from the example set by Horace Alexander, whose photograph was prominently displayed in Quaker House, New Delhi, during John and Erica Linton's tenure there as Quaker representatives in India. John Linton's period of service had opened him to

Indian religious traditions and so he could see the limitations of claims that a single religion was uniquely true. Accordingly, in 1977, after his return to England, John Linton gave a talk to a Quaker group, the Seekers' Association, which was subsequently published in article form as 'Quakerism as Forerunner'. Linton wrote:

What I had found particularly difficult about the Christian claim to be unique was the geographical limitation of Christendom. The same applied of course to other religions claiming uniqueness. Most people are Christian because they happen to have been born in a Christian country; if one had been born in India, one would probably have been a Hindu, or in Indonesia a Muslim. Consequently it seemed to me nonsense to claim absolute Truth for any one religion such as Christianity. Otherwise, why did the good God condemn large parts of the globe to ignorance, superstition and, according to the more orthodox, an extremely uncomfortable life after death, while reserving the knowledge of the truth and salvation mainly for natives of Europe and America? Could the knowledge of the true religion really be a matter of accident?[61]

As a direct consequence of this article the Quaker Universalist Group [QUG] was established in the UK, soon followed by the Quaker Universalist Fellowship in America. To quote from the Quaker Universalist Fellowship's website:

There are many paths toward a truth that lies beyond the confines of any single religious doctrine. No one faith has a monopoly of the way to truth. Seekers must find their own paths, assisted by the search of others.[62]

At the same time Linton distinguished between syncretism and synthesis and articulated the imperative as being to 'create a synthesis of Eastern and Western thinking, of intellect and intuition'. In 'Quakerism as forerunner', John Linton wrote:

> What I envisage for Quakerism to become is a meeting-place for spiritual seekers of all faiths or none, where they can worship or meditate, as they feel drawn. It will be a world-wide religion, without any particular bias, Christian or otherwise, but enshrining the supreme truths of all religions.[63]

During the years that followed, *The Friend* published the polarised views of universalist and Christocentric Friends. *Quaker Faith and Practice* reprints Alastair Heron's, Ralph Hetherington's and Joseph Pickvance's careful response in 1994 to this sometimes pained and painful exchange:

> The ferment of thought in this post-war period has produced a wide variety of beliefs in our Religious Society today and not a little misunderstanding on all sides. Intolerance has reared its head. Some Friends have voiced objections to the use of Christian language in meetings for worship and for business; others have been told that there is no place for them in our Religious Society if they cannot regard themselves as Christians. It has become quite customary to distinguish between 'Christians' and 'universalists' as if one category excluded the other.

The writers continued:

> The situation has led many Friends to suppose that universalist Friends are in some way set over against Christocentric Friends. This is certainly not the case. Universalism is by definition inclusivist, and its adherents accept the right to free expression of all points of view, Christocentric or any other. Indeed, in London Yearly Meeting there are

many universalists whose spiritual imagery and belief are thoroughly Christocentric.

Alastair Heron, Ralph Hetherington and Joseph Pickvance found assurance in the writings of Quakerism's founding fathers:

From the beginning the Quaker Christian faith has had a universal dimension. George Fox saw the Light 'shine through all' and he identified it with the divine Light of Christ that 'enlightens every man that comes into the world' (John 1: 9). He pointed out, as did William Penn in greater detail, that individuals who had lived before the Christian era or outside Christendom and had no knowledge of the Bible story, had responded to a divine principle within them. In these terms, all Quaker Christians are universalists. Obedience to the Light within, however that may be described, is the real test of faithful living.[64]

A few years later the Swarthmore Lecture Committee invited me to give, in 2003, 'a lecture on interfaith issues, looking at questions of what truth is and how different truths relate and talk to one another'. As a result, I devoted considerable thought not only to preparing the required book, which I titled *Interfaith Pilgrims*,[65] but also to responding to Friends' consequent invitations to address related issues in meetings up and down the UK. Amongst other ideas, I shared my realisation of the ways in which a commitment to understanding other people and their faiths is helpful in developing and understanding one's own experience of religious faith and identity. So, the Hindu and Sikh traditions had presented me with ways of understanding that I could fruitfully apply to myself and I commended to others the effort to 'look through other people's lenses', lenses that are inseparable from the language and concepts that they deploy. As I will be outlining later, I suggested that it can be illuminating to examine our own experience through the lens of an Indic concept, such as *dharma,* rather than simply looking at others through the lenses of more familiar concepts, such as 'belief', 'religion', 'culture' and so on.

Friends' insights into how faiths relate to each other, as well as what enhances our personal pilgrimages, tend to stem from personal experience of a particular faith – in the case of American Friend Martha Dart, and British Friends Marjorie Sykes, John Linton, Margot Tennyson and Stephanie Ramamurthy, this was the predominantly Hindu tradition of India. In the case of many other Friends today, it is Buddhism.

Chapter 7: Buddhists

The writer Anne Bancroft has drawn insights from both Buddhism and Quakerism. She grew up in the English Quaker village of Jordans and wrote extensively on spirituality – especially women's, as well as editing the Buddhist Society's publication, *The Middle Way*. In her pamphlet, published by the Quaker Universalist Group, she identified parallels between the spiritual journeys of both Siddhartha Gautama, the Buddha, and (two thousand years later) George Fox. She also highlighted the difference between what they found and she emphasised that 'There are differences between Quakers and Buddhists and these differences should not be papered over in a well-meant attempt at "oneness" (all religions are at heart one) but should be looked at directly and celebrated as new insights, leading to a richer, fuller life'.[66] Nonetheless, Bancroft suggested that the two paths shared a common goal 'in the basic essential – how we should live our lives'. As she explained: 'This "how" encompasses moral, ethical behaviour and our responsibility and compassion for others.'[67] She commented on how widespread it has become for Quakers to combine Buddhist practices with their Quaker way of life.

Certainly, liberal Friends sometimes acknowledge that Buddhist teaching complements Quakerism by providing a useful toolkit for disciplined meditation. For some Friends Buddhist-style meditation stills their minds as part of their daily routine. Engagement with Buddhism gives some people a stepping-stone towards Quakerism and it offers them a continuing supplement. While some Quakers practise meditation during Meeting for Worship, for others this is a far cry from the corporate, worshipful waiting that is intrinsic to Quaker worship and their own more traditionally Christian style of praying. In Anne Bancroft's words 'Quakers have their own meditation and mindfulness in the stillness of a gathered Meeting and the wisdom of Ministry'.[68]

For Peter Taylor, by contrast, Zen (with its heightened awareness of one's breathing and how to hold one's body and sit) provides an answer to the problem of how to meditate in Quaker meetings.[69] In Taylor's view recognising in Zen one's True Nature and, through Quaker processes, coming to a decision are both exercises in understanding our egos and, ultimately, easing our suffering by releasing them. Taylor (or Bub-In, his Buddhist name) was brought up in an American Quaker family and subsequently inducted into the Jogye order of Korean Buddhism.

For Jim Pym ('a Buddhist and a Quaker', who was for many years the manager of the bookshop at Friends House in London), the journey has been from his Roman Catholic upbringing to Buddhism and then to Quakerism. Pym writes eloquently from his long experience of Buddhism and Quakerism and notes the value that many Friends derive from Buddhist meditation techniques. But he cautions against letting these take over the whole of one's time in meeting for worship:

> I know Friends who are so entranced by meditation practice that they forget or ignore the wonder of Quaker worship. This is sad. I have seen such Friends sit in meeting in meditation posture on the floor, obviously giving their whole attention to their breathing or whatever practice of meditation they are involved in... It becomes obvious that they are not surrendering to the grace of the shared Inward Light which is God's gift in Meeting, and are trying to achieve everything by their own efforts.[70]

Sallie King, an American Friend and professor of philosophy and religion, who has written extensively on socially engaged Buddhism, suggests that both Quakerism and Buddhism are tools or vehicles: they do not possess the Truth but, to use a Buddhist image, are both like a finger that points towards the moon, rather than being the moon itself. King detects a strong similarity between the Buddha Nature (every sentient being's potential to be a Buddha) and the Light Within of Quakerism.[71] Each provides a basis for religious pluralism. In both traditions, King emphasises, religious truth is not doctrinal let alone creedal, it is experiential and, as such, there are no words or concepts that can adequately express Truth. For King, Buddhism and Quakerism are like two languages, they are life-worlds that overlap.[72]

Given the inadequacy of words, it is natural that silence is so highly valued by Buddhists and Quakers alike. Both associate silence with a state of repose which creates ideal conditions for spiritual attainment.[73]

Many Quakers have drawn inspiration from the teachings and personality of Thich Nhat Hanh (1926–2022), the Vietnamese Zen master. In the 1960s, at the height of the Vietnam War, he realised Vietnam's need for the Buddha's teachings in order to counter the hatred and violence. Accordingly, 'Thay', as he was known, established Tiep Hien, the Order of Interbeing, a combined lay and monastic community whose members committed themselves to living mindfully. Of more recent years, annual 'Mindfully Together Zen-Quaker Retreats' have been occasions for Buddhists and Friends to make friends and share their spiritual paths.[74]

In the 1960s, one extreme response to the Vietnamese War was a spate of self-immolations by protesters prepared to give their lives for the restoration of peace. Starting with the Buddhist monk Thich Quang Duc in 1963, Vietnamese Buddhists burned themselves to death in protest against the persecution of Buddhists by the Catholic president of South Vietnam, Dgo Dinh Diem. In the USA the Buddhists' self-immolations inspired eight people to immolate themselves in protest against the Vietnam

War. One was a 31-year-old Quaker, Norman Morrison, who burned himself to death at the Pentagon in 1965. His action moved the Vietnamese poet, To Huu, to write a poem and it also profoundly affected the US Secretary of Defense, Robert McNamara, who had shaped the USA's war strategy. In his autobiography McNamara stated that Morrison's death was 'a tragedy not only for his family but also for me and the country. It was an outcry against the killing that was destroying the lives of so many Vietnamese and American youth'.[75]

It is salutary to bear in mind as well Quakers' practical support for Buddhist communities that are caught up in conflict. In the case of Myanmar (formerly Burma) the AFSC (which supported Jewish survivors of the Holocaust) is committed to helping people improve their lives and, until 2016, it supported Buddhist monastic schools, which had been for centuries crucial to the education system, to 'promote self-reliance, life skills and critical thinking. Teacher trainings [sic] also engaged monks and abbots in learning about organizational and financial management and giving them effective skills to run schools'.[76]

Chapter 8: Hindus and Jains

The word 'Hindu' appears in *Quaker Faith and Practice*, in a paragraph by Swami Tripurananda (Jonathan Carter):

> Remember Jesus' answer to the woman of Samaria 'Neither on this mountain nor in Jerusalem will you worship the Father... God is spirit, and those who worship him must worship in Spirit and in Truth.' In the depth of meditation, in the gathered meeting we rise above all limitations. Gone are the concepts of Quakerism and Vedanta. Gone are the ideas of being a Christian or a Hindu. All these concepts are valid on their own level. They have their place, but they are transcended when we merge our minds in Spirit. I believe this is what Jesus and all the other World Teachers wanted us ultimately to do.[77]

Here a monk of the Ramakrishna order (who is from a Quaker background) brackets together an episode in St John's Gospel[78] and Vedanta and commends rising above such distinctions by 'merging our minds in Spirit'. Vedanta, and in the case of the Ramakrishna order, Advaita Vedanta, is a centuries-old philosophy that affirms reality as non-dualistic. In other words, everything (despite appearances) is essentially one. The Ramakrishna order promotes the ideas of two Bengali Hindu masters, Vivekananda (mentioned earlier in connection with the 1893 Parliament of Religions) and his spiritual teacher, Ramakrishna Paramahansa.

A mystical convergence between Hindu and Quaker tradition has appealed to Quakers. American Friend Martha Dart found in her encounters with Hindus in India, and their Upanishads (scriptures), a resonance with John Woolman's 'pure principle' and she rejoiced in the light, unity, simplicity and silence that she discovered in Hinduism.[79]

For some Friends – and Stephanie Ramamurthy mentions it on the basis of her experience in her (by marriage) Hindu family[80] – it is Hindus' ready acceptance of there being many spiritual paths which is refreshing and liberating from a western mindset. In his article 'Quakerism as Forerunner', John Linton had said:

So it is not, in my opinion, for Quakers, while admitting the possibility of Truth in other religions, to go on sticking to the assumption of the superiority of the Christian religion.

The only tenable position, it seems to me, is that of Hinduism. Let those who wish follow the way of Christ: others may wish to follow other 'gurus'. As Dr. Radhakrishnan has pointed out, behind all the different formulations of words, the Truth remains the same.[81]

The Hindu tradition is an intertwining of countless paths, each with its own succession of gurus. The Ramakrishna order, dating from the nineteenth century, which Jonathan Carter/ Swami Tripurananda joined, is one of these. Some other guru-led groups see themselves as Hindu-related rather than as Hindu, among them the Brahma Kumaris World Spiritual University. The Brahma Kumaris, though relatively few in number, have a high profile as an international non-governmental organisation of the United Nations. They have attracted individual Quakers, largely because of a shared emphasis on peace and via the meditation courses that Brahma Kumaris offer in local centres. Quaker writer David Cadman provides a sympathetic account of his encounter with their powerfully inspirational spiritual leader Dadi Janaki. David Cadman also alludes briefly to Brahma Kumaris' history and to their millenarian belief in a cyclical succession of ages, from a pure 'golden age' to a degenerate 'iron age' and global catastrophe, ushering in a new golden age which – though he does not say this – may be more problematic for Quakers to accept.[82]

Another Hindu-related (and many would say simply 'Hindu') movement is ISKCON, the International Society for Krishna Consciousness, often called the Hare Krishna Movement. Kim Knott, a Quaker scholar of Religious Studies, engaged with ISKCON devotees and wrote a sympathetic account of the movement.[83] She has shared how 'the invitation that the Hare Krishna movement gave me to pay more attention to my spiritual journey was certainly part of what brought me to Quakerism'.[84]

Like many Hindus, Quakers often use the title 'Mahatma' (great soul) for one outstanding Hindu in particular, the political leader, Mohandas Gandhi (1869–1948). Gandhi's emphasis on peace and on non-violent protest chimed profoundly with Quakers' own peace testimony. The Quaker philosopher Margaret Chatterjee has written of how a commitment to reconciliation and negotiation united Gandhi and Quakers in India and of 'the inner story of congruence of many of Gandhi's ideas with Quaker religious thought'.[85] Over the decades, a loving esteem for Gandhi has connected many Quakers and Hindus. Prakash Tandon, a Punjabi Hindu (and former director of Unilever in India), included in his autobiography an affectionate description of Hay's Farm, a Quaker guesthouse, below Pendle Hill, recording his sense of peace there and the fact that Gandhi had once visited.[86] Gandhi himself stayed at Woodbrooke in 1931 and he referred warmly to his Quaker friends, notably Horace Alexander.

What fewer Quakers detect is the much more critical attitude towards Gandhi in some Indian communities, and especially among Dalits, whose families have for centuries suffered marginalisation, oppression and stigma from higher-caste Hindus. Dalits look up to a fellow Dalit, Dr B. R. Ambedkar, rather than to Gandhi, as the champion of their rights. Ambedkar was a jurist who headed the committee that drafted independent India's constitution and, in fact, after renouncing Hinduism he established a Dalit Buddhist movement. In accordance with the Quaker testimony to justice and equality, the American scholar Eleanor Zelliot devoted her life to researching and publishing on the Dalits of Ambedkar's state, Maharashtra. In the introduction to their two-volume tribute to Zelliot, the authors explain:

> In some measure as a result of her Quaker background, Zelliot has single-mindedly 'spoken truth to power' through her work. That is, rather than seeking merely to study passively and objectively the 'others' who have been the focus of her work, Zelliot has sought to involve herself in their plight, their misery, and their hope, and she has used her position and her writing to advocate their cause.[87]

In an email Zelliot wrote 'My studying Dr B.R. Ambedkar and the Untouchable Movement is directly related to my being a Quaker and involved in American matters of race from early adolescence'.[88]

In my own case, my involvement in Hindu studies made me aware of how much we ourselves and our religious worldview are shaped and conditioned by our family and circumstances. The term *sanskar* (which can be translated as conditioning or polishing, and also means a 'rite of passage') opened my eyes to the many ways in which people are in fact 'culturally Christian'. They may not regard themselves or describe themselves as Christian but, in Britain at least, the annual holidays for Christmas and Easter, and the tendency for Sundays to be non-working days are among many norms that shape our expectations differently from if we were living in, for example, Islamic or Buddhist countries. It is refreshing to look at Quakers and others through the lens of *sanskar* rather than, say, the familiar English language of 'beliefs and practices' and to ask what our own processing has been.[89]

I have also commended thinking in terms of not only 'religion' and 'faith' but of *dharma*, (which is often translated as 'religion'). For Hindus, *dharma* carries a sense of duty and of what behaviour is appropriate. It conveys an awareness that everyone's responsibilities will differ according to such factors as gender, social positioning and relative seniority. Hindus, I realised, are not unique in assuming that there are differences in what is acceptable or expected behaviour for a school child, an elder son, a daughter-in-law, a mother-in-law, a grandfather.[90]

Gurdial Mallik, a friend of Gandhi and of the visionary poet and educationist Rabindranath Tagore, was the first Hindu to be accepted as a member of the Society of Friends. In the *Friends Bulletin of Pacific Yearly Meeting of Friends* he wrote how when he applied for membership he was initially told that first he must convert to Christianity, a requirement that he could not understand:

> For in the ultimate, each of us is, first, a disciple of the Divine and only afterwards a fellow-pilgrim of all the other Seekers of the Eternal Truth…
>
> That is why neither in the Light, which we envision or worship, nor in the silence, through which we try to contact the Light, is there any sense of separateness, such as the Christian and the Hindu, the Moslem and the Jew. For in Him we are all basically one beneath all forms of thought and fetishes and philosophies and formularies.[91]

Before and since Mallik, others too have identified themselves as Hindu Quakers. One was P.C. (Poornachandra) Sirkar (or Sarkar) of Calcutta who described himself as 'a Hindu Quaker, by race a Hindu and by grace a Quaker'.[92] After learning as a child to worship the Hindu deity Shiva he had become 'an enthusiastic disciple of Christ' and then in 1891 found his spiritual home among Quakers.[93] He hoped to share with others the ways in which 'the insights of the Gita might be related to the Quaker principles of "peace and public righteousness"'.[94]

Another Quaker Hindu is Ashok Jashapara[95] who has reminded Quakers of early glitches in Quaker-Hindu understanding. London Yearly Meeting in 1861 was unwelcoming and unfriendly to an Indian couple who had come to Quakerism and visited London at their own expense to seek help and support for their missionary work. Twenty years later, Samuel Baker, a Quaker missionary was appalled at what seemed to him the ignorance and wickedness of Hindus. By contrast, Jashapura described his own wedding, a Meeting for Worship in which Hindu and Christian elements combined. He suggests that it is easier for 'polytheistic' Hindus to accept Christianity, though presumably not the claims to uniqueness that are intrinsic to many Christians' belief, than for monotheistic Christians to accept Hindu tradition. Jashapura notes 'pockets of racial prejudice within our Meetings'[96] and suggests 'looking for similarities rather than differences'.

One deep influence on Gandhi's commitment to non-violence came from Jainism. Many Jains identify themselves as Hindu – in certain contexts at least – and, like Buddhism, the Jain faith is indeed closely related to the Hindu tradition in its history and concepts. Mahavira, the twenty-fourth of the Tirthankaras (Jains' spiritual masters, literally founders of fords), lived about 600 BCE, a century or so before Gautama Buddha. Although there has been little interaction between Quakers and Jains, some observers have detected parallels. In particular, they have noted, firstly, that Jain *dharma* is to avoid harming other creatures. (Jains are expected to be strictly vegetarian and not to fight, although some have in fact served in the army.) Secondly, rather like nineteenth-century Quakers, Jains have a reputation for being successful urban businesspeople. (They could not be farmers as farming inevitably involves damage and destruction of other life forms.) As Balwant Nevaskar (who wrote a book on the subject) explains, in his view at least, both Jains and Quakers flourished, adopting a means of earning a living that fitted comfortably with their religious convictions.[97]

Chapter 9: Sikhs

My own Quaker path has been irradiated (to echo Douglas Steere's phrase) by my immersion in yet another Indic faith community, the Sikh community. Quaker contact with Sikhs has occurred mainly outside India, and only got underway with the substantial migration of Sikhs to the UK in the second half of the twentieth century. Sikhs are now the fourth largest faith community in the UK, after Christians, Muslims and Hindus – a higher percentage than the similar number of Sikhs in the USA. Whilst most Sikh-Quaker encounters are more informal, some result from the formation of local interfaith groups.

In the 1970s in Patiala, in the Indian state of Punjab, Dharam Singh, a Sikh academic in Punjabi University, questioned me about Quakerism. He subsequently highlighted the convergences that he detected with his own faith tradition. For instance, both traditions 'put equal emphasis on the sacredness of every part of life'.[98] Gopinder Kaur Sagoo, a Sikh educationist and writer in Birmingham (UK), finds another resemblance – this time between the active volunteering of an influential Sikh devotional organisation, the Guru Nanak Nishkam Sevak Jatha, and Birmingham's Civic Gospel, an approach to urban regeneration in which, in the nineteenth century, 'Non-Conformist groups such as the Quakers played an instrumental role'.[99]

Owen Cole, an educationist who joined the Religious Society of Friends late in life, wrote extensively about Sikhs. After quoting from the Guru Granth Sahib the words of Guru Nanak, Sikhs' first Guru, 'There is light among all, and that light is God's self which pervades and enlightens everyone',[100] Cole commented 'Among Christians only the Quakers and some mystics might feel able to support this belief'.[101]

Another Quaker, Kathryn Lum, who conducted ethnographic studies of Sikhs, noted among both Sikhs and Quakers an emphasis on simplicity, service, equality and collective worship. Certainly, the resonances between the Quaker testimonies and intrinsic Sikh values are striking. For example, the founding master's, Guru Nanak's, dictum on truth is often inscribed in gurdwaras (Sikh places of worship): 'Highest is truth, but higher still is truthful living.'[102] At the same time, like Eleanor Zelliot, Lum's concern with equality and justice contributed to her concern for and research among Ravidasis, a community that has often been marginalised and stigmatised by higher-caste Sikhs.

Of course, there are some clear differences of emphasis between Quakers and Sikhs, and not only the difference in ethos between a Christian denomination that originated in a western, English-speaking society and a community that evolved largely within Punjab's patriarchal and caste-based society. In particular, both Quakers and Sikhs believe in coming to the rescue of those who are suffering oppression and persecution, but Quakers more steadfastly adhere to non-violent strategies (although not all Quakers were pacifists in the two World Wars). Moreover, courageous Sikh campaigners bore violence without retaliation during the Akali protests against corrupt management of their historic gurdwaras early last century. Sikhs, however, quote the words of their tenth Guru, Guru Gobind Singh (1666–1708), to Aurangzeb, the Mughal emperor that, when all other means have failed, it is right to draw the sword. Guru Gobind Singh wrote his Zafarnama (letter of victory) in Persian verse and it is part of a respected compilation known as Dasam Granth (the volume of the tenth Guru), which is second in importance only to Sikhs' hallowed scripture, Guru Granth Sahib.

While Quakers stress their commitment to non-violent conflict resolution and challenge militarism, Sikhs are unequivocally proud of their tradition of military prowess. Guru Gobind Singh initiated his Khalsa brotherhood, a nucleus of committed Sikhs who bear five external indicators of their faith, including a (usually very short) sword. The ideal Sikh is described as a *sant-sipahi* (a saint-soldier or warrior saint). This can be interpreted as an image motivating every Sikh to balance spirituality with an alert preparedness for active service. Indeed, the Sikh emphasis on combining *seva* and *simran* (voluntary social service and remembrance of the divine) comes close to Quaker commitment to expressing one's deepest insights in practical ways that benefit society. Quakers and Sikhs also share a respect for other faiths as well as an image of themselves as being less bound by the ritualism of, respectively, Christians (in the Church of England and other churches) and Hindus. Sikhs and Quakers alike see themselves as champions of justice and equality. The American writer and activist Simran Jeet Singh eloquently affirms the divine light in everyone, however heinous their behaviour may be, leaving no doubt of the common ground between Quakers and Sikhs.

Several Sikh concepts have illuminated my own Quaker journey from new angles, among them the distinction between being a wayward egotist (a *manmukh*) and being a *gurmukh*, a person who is consistently God-focused and altruistic. A formula attributed to Guru Nanak can also be a useful anchor and mnemonic for Quakers no less than Sikhs as it bids us to live contemplatively, industriously and generously.[103]

Chapter 10: Quaker interfaith initiatives

As other sections of this book indicate, as well as individual Quakers' interactions, local and Yearly Meetings too have engaged with people of other faiths. Quakers have also set up groups and committees with an interfaith remit, such as (in the UK) the Quaker Committee for Christian and Interfaith Relations (QCCIR) and the Quaker Universalist Group (QUG) and (in the USA) the Christian Interfaith Relations Committee and the Quaker Universalist Fellowship. What's more, Quaker meeting houses continue to provide a welcoming space for members of other faiths.

In the US the Christian Interfaith Relations Committee (CIRC) was founded by liberal (Hicksite) Friends shortly before the 1893 Parliament of Religions in Chicago. Subsequently, in 1902, Friends General Conference was formed from CIRC plus three other Hicksite committees. CIRC 'attempts to promote mutual understanding and to engender closer ties among those of differing religious persuasions'. It expresses Quaker concerns on peace and justice issues and helps express the identity and message of FGC Friends in ecumenical and interfaith contexts.[104]

In the UK the QCCIR published *Quakers and Other Faiths* for use by local meetings and Quaker institutions. It aims to encourage Quaker engagement in interfaith activities and also points out some potential problems and sources of advice, as well as asking whether Quakers have a 'distinctive, even prophetic role'.[105]

Quaker meeting houses play an important part in outreach as they are frequently hired by religious groups for worship and other activities. As early as 1978 a report by the British Council of Churches noted:

Buildings devoted to regular Christian worship should not be made available to acts of worship of other faiths, whilst recognizing the exception of the Meeting Houses and Rooms of the Society of Friends, and the need to consider other possible exceptions on their merits.[106]

Buddhists, Hindus, Jews, Muslims and others voice their appreciation of the buildings' peaceful atmosphere and the absence of symbols and images. Jewish seders and Purim meals,[107] plus various Hindu and Buddhist organisations' meditation sessions, routinely take place in Quaker meeting houses. Sometimes participants feel curious about Quakers, see the notices and Quaker publications, and venture into a meeting for worship.

As imagined by the award-winning Nigerian British playwright Chinonyerem Odimba, a meeting house's outreach might come in the form of a tin of biscuits given to a heavily pregnant Sikh woman who has just been pushed in a supermarket trolley to the Friends Meeting House in Hill Street in Coventry, UK. The woman in question and her husband, Mandeep, are characters in Odimba's 'Faith the Arrival', a multi-location play which was commissioned for Coventry's programme as UK City of Culture.[108] Along with the cast, the spectators too arrive at the Friends Meeting House and hear that Quakers 'believe light is in every single person' and 'Quakers want to live simply'.

In at least one instance, a Quaker meeting house has been sold to the local Sikh community. In the early 1970s Sikhs in Barking (East London) began meeting in the former Quaker hall, where Elizabeth Fry, the nineteenth-century prison reformer, had once preached. (She was subsequently buried in Friends' Burial Ground, now Quaker Gardens, in Barking.) Among the exterior reliefs on the imposing new Sri Guru Singh Sabha gurdwara is a carving of Elizabeth Fry, next to her contemporary, the Sikhs' hero, the Lion of Punjab, Maharajah Ranjit Singh. Incongruous though this juxtaposition may seem, it is worth remembering that Ranjit Singh's lively curiosity meant that he quizzed the westerners who visited him, including the Governor-General's sisters, Fanny and Emily Eden, about the Christian religion. It could be argued too that his promotion of education was itself a social reform.

Sometimes adherents to other faiths take part in meetings for worship. Quakers' vocal ministry may refer to scriptures other than the Bible, and some Quakers may draw inspiration and insight from non-Christian sources in their silent worship. In some meetings in the UK, a multi-faith Bible, a compilation of material from many religious writings, is placed on the table alongside the Bible and *Quaker Faith and Practice*.

James Priestman from Ealing Meeting in West London reported his individual initiative in *The Friend*. As outreach, he decided to hitch-hike so as to talk about the Quaker testimonies to people he wouldn't normally meet. With Jag, the Sikh driver of an articulated lorry, conversation turned to how Sikhs live out the testimonies of truth, love and community. With Taz, a minicab driver, Priestman chatted about the similarities and differences between Quakerism and Islam, 'the main similarity being the simplicity of worship: no rituals, no priests, and no icons'.[109]

Chapter 11: Baha'is

As Baha'is are fewer in number than Jews, Muslims, Buddhists, Hindus or Sikhs it is unsurprising that Quakers have interacted less with Baha'is than with members of these larger faith communities. Baha'is believe in the unity of God, the unity of religions, the oneness of humanity and they seek world peace and economic justice. Like Quakers they refer to themselves as Friends. In the nineteenth century, the Bab, the revered forerunner of the faith's founder, Bahá'u'lláh, taught (rather like George Fox) that communication with God must be direct, without any priestly intervention. Discovering their common concern with peace and with gender equality, with unity between peoples and between science and religion, individual Baha'i and Quaker representatives have valued contact with each other in interfaith groups.

This mutual esteem goes back at least as far as 1910, when some Bristol Quakers sent an Epistle to 'Abdu'l-Bahá and the followers of Bahá'u'lláh. 'Abdu'l-Bahá was the preferred title of Abbas Effendi (1844–1921), the eldest son of Bahá'u'lláh, the founder of the Baha'i faith, and, though he was a political prisoner for most of this time, 'Abdu'l-Bahá was its head from 1892 to 1921. Following his release in 1908, he visited western countries to speak about the Baha'i faith. An article appeared in *The Friend*, documenting the exchange of appreciative letters between some British Friends and 'Abdu'l-Bahá.[110]

Before reproducing the letters, the article's author leaves readers in no doubt of the resonances between Quaker and Baha'i insights and their shared commitment to promoting peace and equality:

The consciousness of the presence of God in all men, independent of priestly mediation, has led them to a testimony against war, much like our own; and the assertion of brotherhood and liberty is essential with them. They are a body of mystics arising out of the Moslem world, and are sometimes called the Quakers of Persia.[111]

The writer mentions the continuing persecution suffered by Baha'is, their slow moves towards the equality of the sexes, their monogamy and 'trying to drop the veil and educate women'.

In reply to the Bristol Friends' letter 'Abdu'l-Bahá wrote:

Convey to them my salutations. Tell them that the Spirit is encompassing and surrounding all. It is holy. It is sanctified from attachment to a special place. It is present everywhere and at every time. It exists in all places, yet is place-less.[112]

A copy of 'Abdu'l-Bahá's full letter was then forwarded to John W. Graham, the Clerk of Lancashire and Cheshire Quarterly Meeting. Graham read it out to Friends gathered in Bolton on 19 January 1911 and was instructed to reply to 'Abdu'l-Bahá. Great care was taken – Edward A. Browne, the University of Cambridge's Professor of Persian, translated Friends' letter into Persian and it was 'addressed under cover for safety to someone else, in Alexandria'. In their letter, the members of Lancashire and Cheshire Quarterly Meeting expressed their gladness 'to hear of those in other lands to whom the indwelling spirit has been so mightily revealed, showing to you and to us that when we draw near to one another we draw near to God and that in the happy recognition of human fellowship we find the bond which makes us one in the Eternal, in spite of the diversity of race and language and the externals of belief'. The Lancashire and Cheshire Friends also expressed their solidarity with Baha'is in their suffering: 'Our hearts go out to you under the fire of persecution which you are undergoing, such as fell upon our forefathers 250 years ago.' Stressing their spiritual affinity, the letter concluded:

Though both you and we may seem, to our critics who belong to Churches of elaborate doctrine and established ritual, to leave out much which to them is precious, we believe that we hold the absolute and simple religion which places no intermediary between God and men.[113]

'Abdu'l-Bahá's prompt reply to Lancashire and Cheshire Friends was translated from Persian to English in London in April 1911. It began 'He is God! O Heavenly Friends!' He thanked God that 'such an assembly is organised which renders service to the unity of the world of humanity, and seeks equality among all men'. 'Abdu'l-Bahá pointed out that Baha'is 'do not consider anyone as an enemy' and 'hope that the spirituality of these precepts... make the five continents of the world as one continent and its different nations as one nation and the rival religions as one religion...'[114]

Then, on 12 January 1913, 'Abdu'l-Bahá addressed Quakers in person. The meeting took place in the meeting house in St Martin's Lane in London and, thanks to his anonymous stenographer and to the meticulous diary of his translator, Ahmad Sohra, we can visualise the setting and read online his message to his audience. 'Abdu'l-Bahá told Friends

about one thousand years ago a society was formed in Persia called the Society of Friends, who gathered together for silent communion with the Almighty. Their philosophy was that of the illuminati, or followers of the inner light. Their meetings were held in silence, turning their faces to the Source of Light...[115]

He assured his hearers that 'their societies still exist' and went on, 'These people, who are called "Followers of the Inner Light", attain to a superlative degree of power, and are entirely freed from blind dogmas and imitations.'[116]

'Abdu'l-Bahá's message to the Friends meeting in the St Martin's Lane meeting house was titled 'The Meditative Faculty'. 'Abdu'l-Bahá explained:

Bahá'u'lláh says there is a sign from God in every phenomenon. The sign of the intellect is contemplation, and the sign of contemplation is silence; because it is impossible for man to do two things at the same time – he cannot both speak and meditate. It is an axiomatic fact that while you meditate you are speaking with your own spirit. In that state of mind you put certain questions to your spirit, the spirit answers, the light breaks forth, and reality is revealed... Through the faculty of meditation man attains to eternal life; through it he receives the breath of the Holy Spirit – the bestowal of the Spirit is given in reflection and meditation... Through it, he receives Divine inspiration, through it he partakes of Heavenly Food. Meditation is the key for opening the doors of mysteries...[117]

To set the scene, Ahmad Sohrab, provided a glimpse of the Quaker meeting in which this address occurred and the self-effacing ease with which 'Abdu'l-Bahá had adapted to Quaker convention:

The church was extremely quiet. On the platform two men and two women were sitting. The Master very quietly entered the church. No one was speaking. The Master sat down and closed his eyes in meditation. I asked the woman who conducted us whether this is the time to speak. She said yes. It was 11.45. I told the Master. As soon as he arose from his seat, from another corner a woman prompted by the Spirit got up and began to talk. The Master sat down and waited until the lady began and talked for about 5 minutes. Then finishing her points she sat down. Our Beloved then got up and gave a beautiful address on the Meditative Faculty. [118]

The outbreak of the First World War put an end to 'Abdu'l-Bahá's European travels and, it would seem, to communication with British Quakers. Sadly, the persecution of Baha'is in some Muslim countries, and especially in Iran, has continued and many more Baha'is have moved abroad.

A century after the mutually endorsing exchange of letters and 'Abdu'l-Bahá's address, the Quakerism of liberal Friends has become more and more liberal, while the Baha'i community, in America at least, shows signs of increasing 'fundamentalism'[119] with an emphasis on the infallibility of their scripture and of the Bahai's' Universal House of Justice, the international governing council whose guidance ensures unity of thought and action in the Baha'i community worldwide. Baha'is' moral code is inflexible: same-sex partnerships are forbidden, for example, and as a result some young American Baha'is are regretfully relinquishing their membership.

Chapter 12: Indigenous religions

Just as William Penn and John Woolman met and listened to Native Americans, so Quakers in New Zealand/Aotearoa and Australia have been sensitive to Māori and Aboriginal experience. In 1993 New Zealand Quakers were officially named Te Hāhi Tūhauwiri (those who stand shaking in the wind of the spirit) and their book of discipline introduces the reader to John Silvanus Cotterill (1819–1843) from Bath in the UK who came out to New Zealand:

> We have it on the best authority that he took no part in the affray, except as an unarmed peacemaker; that during the whole of his sojourn in New Zealand, he was on the best terms with the natives; and the very last letter received from him mentions the pleasure he experienced in having acquired sufficient of the native language to be enabled to converse with the 'Maories' on religious subjects.[120]

As a recent example, Quaker responses to Māori understanding of the connectedness of people through their human genealogies, and also with the rest of nature, appear in an exchange of views in 2016. New Zealand Quaker, Murray Short, relates:

> In an article that appeared in the Aotearoa New Zealand Friends Newsletter following the 2016 Quaker Yearly Meeting, a comment was made about the epistle of that Meeting referring to 'honouring your ancestors' including 'the volcanoes that form the land here in Tamaki Makaurau/ Auckland'. While one Friend wrote that the epistle was 'concerning', and that 'those Friends especially in Africa who had not long been converted from ancestor worship and animism' would be 'shaken by reading this', some other Friends were supportive:

Animism is belief in a dynamic supernatural power which animates the material world. Many Quakers believe in that of God in all things (panentheism) which is not very different from animism. Rather than condemn animism we can learn from it, to treasure the natural world. Respect for volcanoes comes into this.

For myself, I can adopt the spirituality of Aotearoa with deep respect for the land, especially that which moves beneath my feet in the form of earthquakes/Rūaumoko and the amazing volcanoes that dominate Te Ika a Māui.[121]

In Māori mythology Ruaumoko is god of earthquakes, volcanoes and seasons and is the youngest son of the sky father and the earth mother. Te Ika a Māui is New Zealand's North Island. Amongst Aotearoa/New Zealand Friends there is a growing perspective that the foundational Quaker view of 'That of God in everyone' is better phrased as 'That of God in everything'.[122]

Above all, New Zealand Quakers are committed to working to redress the injustices perpetuated by the non-Māori majority's disregard for the 1840 Treaty of Waitangi (Te Tiriti o Waitangi) between the British Crown and Māori. For example:

Some Meetings are allied with the Parihaka Network to support the people of Parihaka, to educate the wider community about suffering caused by the unlawful sacking of their village, the imprisonment of their men and violation of women and girls in November 1881, and to promote the values upon which Parihaka was built.

Individual Friends have upheld the cause of Parihaka, and Meetings have organised commemorations to remember the grave injustice and to support the call for recognition of it by the Crown. With the Crown apology being given in 2017, celebrations continue in recognition of the peaceful non-violent resistance observed by the people of Parihaka in 1881 and since.[123]

Out of this same concern for justice and equality, Quaker Service Australia has undertaken small projects to support Australia's indigenous population. The Indigenous Concerns Committee of Quakers Australia guides Friends to seek ways to 'come into right relationship' with Aboriginal peoples. A longing for Aboriginal people to experience justice and equality rings through entries in Australia Yearly Meetings' book of discipline, *This We Can Say: Australian Quaker Life, Faith and Thought*. Inseparably from their distress at Aboriginals' disinheritance, oppression and exploitation, Australian Friends also acknowledge a shared spirituality. So, a section entitled 'Facing the challenges of time and place' includes Susannah Brindle's words:

> The Earth continues to speak to me in many voices and I am coming to sense its yearning for conscious communion with a humanity that has for so long almost severed its life-connection... The deeper I enter into this Earth-communion the more keenly I feel the dispossession of the Bjadjawurung people. Recently I faced my territorial paranoia and asked their permission for us to live on this land, making it clear that if 'Eldamar' was a good 'sit-down place' they should feel free to have access to it – As they tell me the Dreaming stories associated with this sacred place, I begin to experience what it is like to live in a land which has been sung (a little) into life. I feel I no longer cling so tentatively to its surface. Some of its wisdom has entered into me and this connectedness gives me a greater sense of identity and integrity as a human being.[124]

Susan Addison reported a meeting in 2001 with Mary Graham, a Kombumerri person (i.e., from an Aboriginal community from Queensland's Gold Coast). The common ground that Addison and Graham identified included:

Appreciation of silence
Sense of awe in nature
Caring for the land
Respect for the whole person, including those who are different
Deep sharing gathered in circles

Their list continued:

Simplicity through non-hierarchical, non-competitive, non-materialistic society
Decision-making by general agreement and concord
No priests as intermediaries – the individual contributes his or her abilities or gifts for the benefit of the whole society
Spirituality permeates the whole of life – no holy days, everyday life is sacred.[125]

Another Australian Quaker, Adrian Glamorgan, shared this insight:

Dwelling in the deep silence the spirit may speak in its immediate way, or bide its time. Conceivably it may happen in special places writ in the landscape, or through Aboriginal voices, expressing aspects of this divine spirit which Friends uphold and are now beginning to hear in an Australian setting. How we discern such a meeting of cosmologies, and test the labour to justly share, may be one of the deepest mysteries our generation is led to celebrate.[126]

I will be glad to hear of liberal Quaker engagement with African primal religion. One scholar who introduced readers to African (and other continents') indigenous faith traditions was John Ferguson who became a Quaker only shortly before his death in 1989.

The UK's indigenous, pre-Christian beliefs and practices were pejoratively called 'pagan' and, as already mentioned, with regard to the names of the days of the week, early Quakers rejected their 'heathen' association with the sun and moon and northern European gods such as Woden and Thor. Likewise, the names of some months were rejected because they evoked Mars and other Roman deities. As a result, from early in their history Quakers referred to days and months not by their usual names but by their number. Accordingly, 1 June was first of fourth month. In 1752, in Britain and North America, the Gregorian calendar replaced the Julian calendar and January replaced March as the first month of the year. This meant not only that 1 June was now first of sixth month but also that the previously acceptable names, September, October, November and December were acceptable no longer. These Latin names indicated what had been, up till that point, the seventh, eighth, ninth and tenth months of the year. So, in Quaker usage, they now became ninth, tenth, eleventh and twelfth month.

Of course, Quakers nowadays are comfortable referring to days and months by name. Like many others, they are critical of the consumerism that dominates Christmas, but they are rather less likely than their predecessors to completely distance themselves from it as a pagan celebration. What's more, the name Pagan (with an initial capital letter) is confidently claimed by the growing number of people who are drawn to a Goddess spirituality and to a way of being that honours the Earth and its seasons and perpetuates rites that evoke the pagan tradition of centuries past.

Not only has liberal Friends' antipathy to vestiges of pre-Christian pagan belief and practice ebbed away but, in Britain and North America, some Quakers have been attracted to Pagan affirmation of the 'Goddess' while Pagans have been attracted by Quakers' silent worship and freedom from creeds and formal doctrine. The Quaker Goddess network links people whose spiritual journeys overlap two paths – a love for Goddess spirituality, stories and ritual, and the practice of silent Quaker worship, together with the disciplined Quaker way of making decisions. Heather Sowers, who identifies with Wicca, has shared her understanding, as a 'Quitch' (Quaker witch) in 'Quakerism, Earth-Centred Spirituality and the Goddess'.[127] Giselle Vincent[128] provides an introduction to Quagans, most of them women, who fuse Quaker and Pagan practices and insights. Quaker dislike of creeds and formal doctrine attracts Pagans who tend to be white, middle class, middle-aged women.

Chapter 13: Humanists

While individual Quakers have felt spiritually nourished by immersing themselves to varying degrees in world faiths and religious traditions of many sorts and have opened themselves to new light from these, some liberal Friends are not only uncomfortable with expressing their faith in traditionally Christian terms but also find God-language uncomfortable. Especially for Friends who are no longer theist, there is a clear affinity with humanism.

Humanists and Quakers acknowledge that they share a commitment to living out certain values. To quote the American Humanist Association:

> Quaker focuses on peace, integrity, community and equality resonate closely with humanism. We stand on common ground. Let us begin to walk together. Let these principles and practices be the meeting place of the Quaker and the humanist life stance.[129]

Although this is controversial, humanism no less than Quakerism has, arguably, been shaped in a Christian cultural context. Many Quakers may well agree with the humanist view that religions are created by human beings. For non-theist Friends, that is Quakers who do not find the concept of God helpful, humanism's rejection of belief in God is unproblematic. However, humanists' atheism is a significant point of difference from theist Friends, who are comfortable talking about God as active in their lives, even if they prefer to use alternative terms such as 'Spirit'.

Nonetheless, for David Boulton, who subsequently edited the book *Godless for God's Sake; Nontheism in Contemporary Quakerism*:

There is no meaningful conflict between the human-centred and the God-centred. If God is no more (but, gloriously, no less) than a projection of our highest and deepest values, and if these must be human values (because no other form of life has created and articulated them), God-centredness just becomes one way, a religious way, of talking about being human.[130]

For their part, humanists suggest that non-theist Friends may wish to self-identify as both humanist and Quaker.[131]

Chapter 14: Looking back, looking forward

The story of Quakers and other faiths is a story of continuity and change. Many Quakers would emphasise the importance of continuing to uphold the testimonies to peace, simplicity, community, justice and equality and truth and integrity. At the same time, it is salutary to acknowledge that some convictions have changed over the years: the earliest Quakers' egalitarian outlook had faded by the eighteenth century when Friends in New England held a testimony to inequality and British Friends, too, probably regarded social hierarchies as ordained by God.[132]

Over the centuries, however, Quakers have maintained their emphasis on openness to new insights and on personal experience, rather than advocating unquestioning and unchanging belief either in scripture or in doctrine. The weekly unprogrammed, largely silent meeting for worship continues to be central to the lives of liberal Friends and they are united too by continuing adherence to their distinctive business method. Quakers in successive generations have been drawn to the mystical aspects of other faiths.

Returning to the theme of change – since the initial ferment and fervour in the seventeenth century, Quakers have had decades of quietism and then of high-profile commitment to social reform. The onetime insistence upon marrying only within the Quaker community and Quakers' rejection of the arts are a far cry from present-day norms and attitudes. The more evangelical tenor of London Yearly Meeting a hundred years ago has given way to a more theologically agnostic ethos. In the twentieth century liberal Quakers diverged in their beliefs about Jesus and differed over whether their faith was Christ-centred or not. Now, in the twenty-first century, God too is problematic for a growing number of liberal Friends. Arguably, this greater uncertainty parallels some Anglican theologians' (notably Don Cupitt's) development of a non-realist theology which resulted in the 'sea of faith' network.[133]

In the twentieth century, how best to relate to people of other faith communities became a pressing concern for British and American Quakers who had spent long periods in Asia and for those who encountered people of other faiths who had migrated and settled in their neighbourhoods.

What is observable today is that, among liberal friends, some 'regard the Quaker way as a distinct religious tradition, rooted in Christianity but open to new light' while, over the past forty years, others have come to regard it 'as a more neutral framework within which individuals can follow their own spiritual journey drawing on a wide range of sources of inspiration'.[134] Among these Friends a few people define themselves as Hindu Quakers, Jewish Quakers etc., and many others find their thinking and devotional practice enriched from other faith traditions. This is not so different from the situation among non-Quaker Christians as a 'significant number of people in Christian countries engage in spiritual practices from Eastern religions like Yoga, Zen Meditation, Tai-Chi',[135] Liberal Quakers are not alone in looking beyond their own tradition for meaning and wellbeing.

Being open to other faiths has meant being open to change, whether it is in matters of belief (some New Zealand Quakers moving towards respecting that of God in everything from that of God in everyone), or in daily life (incorporating yoga or meditation in their spiritual practice), or in the range of spoken ministry during meeting for worship.

And an interesting aside: we have noted in passing, how several scholars whose professional life has been devoted to exploring religions gradually found their own spiritual home among Quakers – in some cases near the end of their lives. This was certainly true of one British interfaith advocate, John

Ferguson, an academic with experience of serving in Nigeria. Ferguson's abundant published work introduced readers to the religions of classical Greece and Rome, to primal religion in Africa and other continents and to many other religions. One of his vigorous recommendations for strengthening interfaith relations was the practice of 'conviviality', in other words, making sure we eat together. In Ferguson's experience sharing meals together was the best way of learning and bonding.

Conviviality is a good note to end on. Quakers and non-Quakers alike can, individually and collectively, both offer and accept more hospitality, alert to one another's needs and sensitivities and able to relax, celebrate and, on occasion, to mourn together.

In official documents reference is increasingly made to 'those of all faiths and none'. Successive censuses, in the UK at least, record a growing number of people who identify with no religion. However, many of them regard themselves as 'spiritual' and believe in God and an afterlife. Quakers' conviviality and openness to others' insights needs to extend beyond those who identify themselves with a faith.

As regards their testimonies, Quakers look set to continue affirming the qualities of simplicity and truth and integrity in others. Friends' dedication to the peace testimony will mean not only concurring with other faiths' endorsement of peace and their encouragement of peace of mind but also supporting their followers in peacemaking and conflict resolution. It is likely that mounting concern for sustainability and green issues will unite activists of all faiths and those who do not identify with any religion. Deep ecology, with its challenge to humans to relate more humbly to the planet's non-human residents, provides its champions with an ethical framework, sense of community and a solidarity with Earth that can take on a mystical character. Here too is a faith for Quakers and others to engage with.

Indeed, it is inseparable from a commitment to justice and equality, a commitment that will always risk distancing members of some communities while bringing others, and their worldviews, closer. It has never been more important, as hosts and guests, to co-operate across any boundaries and to share our doubts as well as our certainties.

References

Chapter 1: Getting started

1   David Boulton (1997) 'The Faith of a Quaker Humanist', Quaker Universalist Group, p.4.

2   See   https//quakerinfo.org/Quakerism/faithandpractice (accessed 2 July 2022) for a definition of each category.

3   See, for example, Anthony Manousos (ed.) (2011) *Quakers and the Interfaith Movement: A Handbook for Peacemakers*, Quaker Universalist Fellowship; Jim Pym (2000) *The Pure Principle: Quakers and Other Faiths*, York: William Sessions Limited; Eva Tucker and Stephanie Ramamurthy (2013) *Signposts: Quakers Exploring Interfaith*, London: The Kindlers; and Quaker Committee for Christian and Interfaith Relations (2015) *Quakers and Other Faiths*, London: Quaker Committee for Christian and Interfaith Relations (QCCIR) of the Yearly Meeting of the Religious Society of Friends (Quakers) in Britain.

Chapter 2: Some early interfaith encounters

4   Letter from Mary Fisher to Thomas Killam, Thomas Aldam & John Killam in LSF Caton MSS vol 1, p. 164, printed in Mabel R. Brailsford (1915) *Quaker Women, 1650–1690*, p.130. Also in *QFP* 19.27.

5   Vlasblom, David (2011) 'Islam in Early Modern Quaker Experience', *Quaker History*, 100 (1), p.1.

6   Samuel Janney (1882 6th edn) *The Life of William Penn with Selections from his Correspondence and Autobiography*, Philadelphia: Friends Book Association, p.44.

7   Jacob Post (1850) *A Popular Memoir of William Penn, Proprietor and Governor of Pennsylvania: Under Whose Wise Administration the Principles of Peace were Maintained in Practice*, London: Charles Gilpin, p.28.

8   *CFP* 227; *QFP* 27.01.

9   Janney (1882) p.246. This seems to reflect a relatively common view at the time. See Brandon Marriott (2015) *Transnational Networks and Cross-Religious Exchange in the Seventeenth-Century Mediterranean and Atlantic Worlds: Sabbatai Sevi and the Lost Tribes of Israel,* Fareham: Ashgate, reviewed by Stuart Masters (2016) in *Quaker Studies,* 21, 2, pp.287–289.

10   Janney (1882) p.241.

11   Janney (1882) p.244.

12   Janney (1882) p.244.

13   John Woolman *QFP* 26.61.

14   This comes from section XVI of Propositions 5 and 6, of the *Apology*, p.127 (in the Quaker Heritage Press version): Robert Barclay and Licia Kuenning (ed.) (2002) *An Apology for the True Christian Divinity*, Glenside, PA: Quaker Heritage Press, p.127.

15   *CFP* 224 and *QFP* 27.05. from Barclay (1678) prop, 10, sect 2: 1678 London edn pp.181–182; 1886 Glasgow edn, pp.194–195. As Stuart Masters pointed out to me, 'early Friends believed in an invisible *ecclesia spiritualis.* So, they accepted that it was possible for there to be members of the one true faith (the people of God in the new covenant dispensation) in all places and cultures, while at the same time condemning all other instructional religions (including all other Christian groups) as fundamentally false or apostate' (email communication 31 August 2022).

16   Meeting for Sufferings minutes IV (1684–1685), 98.

Chapter 3: Interfaith pointers in Quakers' books of discipline

17   Nitoe in *CFP* 89.

18   Tucker and Ramamurthy (2013) pp.32–33.

19   Marjorie Sykes in *CFP* 226 and *QFP* 27.11.

20 Galatians 5:22.

21 Hobling, Margaret (1958) *The Concrete and the Universal* (Swarthmore Lecture), London: George Allen & Unwin; *CFP* 225.

22 John Woolman in *QFP* 27.02.

23 Henry T. Hodgkin *QFP* 27.07.

24 *CFP* 1.05.

25 *QFP* 1.02. 6 and 7.

26 Advices and Queries 12, The Society of Friends (1 Jan. 1964).

Chapter 4: Muslims

27 John Punshon *QFP* 27.08.

28 See http://dannycoleman.blogspot.com/2010/12/quakers-and-sufis.html (accessed 9 July 2022).

29 Manousos 'Becoming a Friend of God: The Path of Sufism and Quakerism' in Manousos (2011) pp.171–176.

30 Manousos 'Islam from a Quaker Perspective' in Manousos (2011) pp.147–170. In a similar spirit another American Quaker, Michael Birkel, Emeritus Professor of Christian Spirituality at Earlham School of Religion, shares insights from conversations with Muslims in this recording https://www.youtube.com/watch?v=4YuWJLaBSxQ (accessed 12 September 2022).

31 Brett Miller-White (2004) 'The Journeyman – the Making of a Muslim Quaker', *Quaker Theology*, 10, pp.1–2.

32 Christopher Bagley (2015) 'Islam Today: A Muslim Quaker's View', QUG pamphlet no 34, QUG Publishing.

33 Lampen, John (2017) *Quaker Roots and Branches*, Alresford: John Hunt Publishing Ltd, p.48.

34, 35 Moheen, Naveed https://quakerspeak.com/video/why-i-am-a-quaker-and-a-muslim/ (accessed 10 July 2022).

36 Qur'an 47.34.

37 Anthony Manousos (2002) 'Islam from a Quaker Perspective', Quaker Universalist Fellowship.

Chapter 5: Jews

38 Tony Stoller (2018) 'The End of the Affair? Examining the Relationship between Quakers and Jews in Britain at the Start of the Twenty-first Century', *Quaker Studies*, 23 (2), pp.239–254.

39 Stuart Masters (2015) 'Abraham's Offspring, Heirs According to the Promise' (Galatians 3.28), *Friends Quarterly*, 4, pp.4–15.

40 See Harvey Gillman (2009) 'Quakers and Jews', *The Friend* https://thefriend.org/article/quakers-and-jews/ (accessed 7 September 2022).

41 Margot Tennyson (1992) *Friends & Other Faiths*, London: Quaker Home Service, p.24.

42, 43 Sue Beardon (2016) 'On being a Jew and a Quaker', *Quaker Voices*, 7, 2, pp.2–6.

44 Lionel Blue frequently referred to this personal milestone. See, e.g., https://www.churchtimes.co.uk/articles/2006/24-november/features/interview-lionel-blue-rabbi-and-broadcaster (accessed 10 July 2022).

45 QCCIR (2015) p.18.

46, 47 *Jewish Chronicle* (2011) 'How Quakers Turned Spiteful', *Jewish Chronicle*, 27 April.

48 Alexander Joffe and Asaf Romirowsky (2015) 'The Quakers, No Friends of Israel', *Wall Street Journal*, 5 November. See also Asaf Romirowsky and Alexander Joffe (2015) 'How the Quakers became Champions of BDS', *Tablet*, 10 November 2017.

49 Brant Rosen (2018) 'Banning the Quakers won't Stop our Struggle for Justice in Israel-Palestine', *+972 Magazine*, 12 January.

50 Shalev Chemi (2018) 'Israel's Blacklisting of Quakers is a Crime against Jewish History', *Haaretz*, 6 January.

51 Harvey Gillman (2017) 'Friends with Jewish Connections', *The Friend*, 27 July.

52 QCCIR (2015) p.3.

Chapter 6: Quaker interfaith approaches

53 Alan Race (2001) *Interfaith Encounter: The Twin Tracks of Theology and Dialogue*, London: SCM Press.

54 John Hick (1990) 'A Philosophy of Religious Pluralism' in Paul Badham (ed.) *A John Hick Reader*, London: Macmillan, 161–177; Hick, John (1995) *The Rainbow of Faiths*, London: SCM, pp.13–16.

55 Damaris Parker-Rhodes (1977) *Truth: A Path not a Possession* (Swarthmore Lecture 1977), London: Quaker Home Service. Quoted in Pym (2000), p.39.

56 See https://www.quakersintheworld.org/quakers-in-action/230/Rufus-Jones (accessed 10 July 2022).

57 Henry T. Hodgkin in *QFP* 27.07.

58 Geoffrey Maw (1997) *Pilgrims in Hindu Holy Land: Sacred Shrines of the Indian Himalayas* (eds Gillian M. Conacher and Marjorie Sykes), York: Sessions.

59 Margot Tennyson (1992) pp.9ff.

60 Douglas V. Steere (1971) *Mutual Irradiation: A Quaker View of Ecumenism*, Pendle Hill Pamphlet no. 175, Pennsylvania, quoted by Margot Tennyson (1992) pp.11ff.

61 John Linton (1979) 'Quakerism as Forerunner', *The Seeker*. Available at: https://qug.org.uk/wp-content/pamphlets/QUGP01-Quakerism_as_Forerunner-LINTON.pdf (accessed 23 July 2022).

62 https://universalistfriends.org/intro.html (accessed 22 July 2022).

63 John Linton (1979).

64 *QFP* 27.04.

65 Eleanor Nesbitt (2003) *Interfaith Pilgrims*, London: Quaker Books.

Chapter 7: Buddhists

66, 67, 68 Anne Bancroft (2008) QUG Pamphlet 33: 'Quakerism and Buddhism: The Cutting Edge'.

69 Peter Taylor https://www.friendsjournal.org/the-zen-of-quakerism/

70 Jim Pym (2000) p.84.

71 See also, in Estella Lovett (2009) 'Buddhists and Quakers', *The Friends Quarterly*, 37, 1, p.36, 'the Buddha mind' is very close to what we call 'that of God in everyone'.

72 King, Sallie (2011) 'A Quaker/Buddhist View of Religious Pluralism' in Manousos (2011).

73 Sandra Bell and Peter Collins (1998) 'Religious Silence: British Quakerism and British Buddhism Compared', *Quaker Studies* 3, pp.1–26.

74 Bradshaw, Harry and Collington, Lesley (2018) 'Zen and Quaker Practice a sharing of spiritual paths and friendship' https://plumvillage.uk/zen-quaker-practice-sharing-spiritual-paths-friendship/ (accessed 25 June 2022).

75 See Sallie King (2000) 'They who Burned themselves for Peace: Quaker and Buddhist Self-Immolation during the Vietnam War', *Buddhist-Christian Studies*, 20, pp.127–150.

76 https://www.afsc.org/office/myanmar-burma (accessed 24 June 2022).

Chapter 8: Hindus and Jains

77 Tripurananda in *QFP* 27.10.

78 John 4. 24.

79 Martha Dart (1989) *To Meet at the Source: Hindus and Quakers*, Pendle Hill Pamphlet 289.

80 Tucker and Ramamurthy (2013) p.50.

81 John Linton (1979) p.3.

82 David Cadman (2005) 'A point of light: Meeting the Brahma Kumaris' available at http://brahmakumaris.info/download/BK%20Academic%20papers/A-Point-of-Light.pdf (accessed 17 April 2022).

83 Kim Knott (1986) *My Sweet Lord: The Hare Krishna Movement*, Wellingborough: Aquarian.

84 Eleanor Nesbitt (2010) 'Interrogating the Experience of Quaker Scholars in Hindu and Sikh Studies: Spiritual Journeying and Academic Engagement', *Quaker Studies*, 14, 2, p.142.

85 Margaret Chatterjee (2005) *Gandhi and the Challenge of Religious Diversity: Religious Pluralism Revisited*, New Delhi: Promilla & Co.

86 Prakash Tandon (1968) *Punjabi Century 1857–1947*, Berkeley: University of California Press, pp. 219–220.

87 M. Bhagavan and A. Feldhaus (eds) (2008) *Claiming Power from Below: Dalits and the Subaltern Question*, New Delhi: Oxford University Press, p.2.

88 Eleanor Zelliot email 6 June 2009.

89 Nesbitt (2003) pp.65–66.

90 Nesbitt (2003) p.43.

91 Gurdial Mallik 1963 Friends Bulletin Pacific Yearly Meeting of Friends, April–May, 31, 4 available at https://archive.org/stream/friendsbulletinp314unse_2/friendsbulletinp314unse_2_djvu.txt (accessed 1 July 2022).

92 Marjorie Sykes (1997) *An Indian Tapestry: Quaker Threads in the History of India, Pakistan & Bangladesh from the Seventeenth Century to Independence*, York: Sessions Book Trust, p.151.

93 Sykes (1997) p.109.

94 Sykes (1997) p.151.

95 Ashok Jashapura (2009) 'Looking at the Light rather than the Lampshade', *The Friends Quarterly*, 37, 1, pp.39–46.

96 Jashapura (2009) p.44.

97 Balwant Nevaskar (1971) *Capitalists without Capitalism: The Jains of India and the Quakers of the West*, Westport: Greenwood.

Chapter 9: Sikhs

98 Dharam Singh (1994) 'Sikhism and Quakerism: An Inter-Faith Enquiry', *The Sikh Review*, Calcutta (December), pp.5–8.

99 Gopinder Kaur Sagoo (2009) 'A Sikh-Inspired Vision for Learning: The Discursive Production of an Ethos by Members of the GNNET Education Trust', unpublished M Res dissertation, University of Birmingham, pp.20, 23.

100 *Adi Granth*, p.663.

101 Owen Cole and Piara Singh Sambhi (1993) *Sikhism and Christianity: A Comparative Study*, Basingstoke: Macmillan, p.198.

102 *Adi Granth*, p.62.

103 The original words are *nam japo, kirat karo, wand chhako*, i.e., repeat God's name, work and share what you earn.

Chapter 10: Quaker interfaith initiatives

104 Manousos (2011).

105 QCCIR (2015) p.103.

106 British Council of Churches (1978) *The Community Orientation of the Church: Final report of the BCC working party on the use of church properties for community activities in multi-racial areas*, London: BCC. p.25.

107 Seder is a special meal for the holiday of Pesach (Passover) and Purim is a holiday commemorating how, as narrated in the biblical Book of Esther, Jews in Persia were saved from being killed.

108 See https//www.youtube.com/watch?v574vJdCB8Yg (accessed 14 June 2022).

109 James Priestman (2022) 'Getting hitched: James Priestman is taken for a ride', *The Friend*, 180, 26: pp.10–12.

Chapter 11: Baha'is

110 (1911) 'Persian Mystic and Friends' Quarterly Meeting', *The Friend*, 5 May.

111 'Persian Mystic', p.184.

112 'Persian Mystic', p.184.

113 'Persian Mystic', p.185.

114 Tennyson (1992) p.6.
115 https://www.bahai.org/library/authoritative-texts/abdul-baha/paris-talks/7#549549309 (accessed 27 July 2022).
116 https://www.bahai.org/library/authoritative-texts/abdul-baha/paris-talks/7#549549309 (accessed 27 July 2022).
117 https://bahai-library.com/pdf/n/nsa-uk_footsteps_abdul-baha_1912.pdf p. 32 (accessed 23 July 2022).
118 https://paintdrawer.co.uk/david/folders/spirituality/bahai/abdulbaha/sohrab-diary-uk-1913.pdf p.146 (accessed 11 July 2022).
119 Juan R.I. Cole (2002) 'Fundamentalism in the Contemporary U.S. Baha'i Community', *Review of Religious Research*, 43, 3, pp.195–217.

Chapter 12: Indigenous religions

120 The Religious Society of Friends (Quakers) Te Hāhi Tūhauwiri (2003) *Quaker Faith and Practice in Aotearoa New Zealand*, Auckland: The Yearly Meeting of the Religious Society of Friends (Quakers) of Aotearoa New Zealand Te Hāhi Tūhauwiri.
121 Murray Short (2021) 'Care for the Planet: Toward a Quaker Story', Yearly Meeting of the Religious Society of Friends (Quakers) of Aotearoa New Zealand/Te Hāhi Tūhauwiri, available at https://quakers.nz/sites/default/files/documents/ANZFNL_2021_07_Supplement.pdf (accessed 3 July 2022) citing Heather List (2016) 'Ancestors and Volcanoes', *Aotearoa New Zealand Friends Newsletter*, 85, 5 Nov, 12; Viola Palmer (2017) 'Responses to "Ancestors and Volcanoes"', *Aotearoa New Zealand Friends Newsletter*, 99, 1, March, 14–15; and Marion Leighton (2017) 'Responses to "Ancestors and Volcanoes"', *Aotearoa New Zealand Friends Newsletter*, 99, 1, March, 15.
122 email from Murray Short 3 July 2022.

123 https://quakers.nz/explore-rapua-%E2%96%BC/faith-action#Parihaka (accessed 3 July 2022).

124 Susannah Brindle (1996) in Australia Yearly Meeting of the Religious Society of Friends (Quakers) Inc. (2003) *This we can Say: Australian Quaker Life, Faith and Thought,* Australia Yearly Meeting of the Religious Society of Friends (Quakers) Inc. 5.50.

125 Susan Addison (2001) in *This we can Say* 5.35.

126 Adrian Glamorgan (1997) in *This we can Say* 5.52.

127 Heather Sowers (2003) 'Quakerism, Earth-Centred Spirituality and the Goddess' in *Friends Journal,* October, 49, 10 pp.25–27.

128 Giselle Vincent (2008) 'Quagans: Fusing Quakerism with Contemporary Paganism' in Pink Dandelion and Peter Collins (eds) *The Quaker Condition: The Sociology of a Liberal Religion,* Newcastle; Cambridge Scholars Publishing, pp.174–191.

Chapter 13: Humanists

129 https//americanhumanist.org/paths/Quakerism/ (accessed 2 July 2022).

130 David Boulton (1997) 'The Faith of a Quaker Humanist', QUG Pamphlet 26.

131 https//americanhumanist.org/paths/Quakerism/ (accessed 2 July 2022).

Chapter 14: Looking back, looking forward

132 I am grateful to Stuart Masters for pointing me to Elizabeth Cazden (2021) '"Within the Bounds of their Consciences": The Testimony of Inequality Among Eighteenth-Century New England Friends' in Robynne Rogers Healey (ed.) *Quakerism in the Atlantic World, 1690–1830,* University Park, PA: Pennsylvania State University Press, pp. 44–64.

133 See https://sofn.org.uk/indexC.html (accessed 10 July 2022). The network's stated aim is to 'explore and promote religious faith as a human creation'.

134 My thanks to Stuart Masters for his insights.

135 Perry Schmidt-Leukel (2009) *Transformation by Integration: How Inter-Faith Encounter Changes Christianity*, London: SCM Press, p.68.

About the author

For many years Eleanor Nesbitt has been a member of Central England Area Meeting in the UK. She is also Professor Emeritus (Religions and Education), University of Warwick. Eleanor grew up in a predominantly Anglican home and married into a Punjabi Hindu family. In 2003 she gave the Swarthmore lecture 'Interfaith Pilgrims'. Many of her other publications are on Sikhs.

Some previous titles

Listening to Hindus (with Robert Jackson) Unwin Hyman, 1990
Hindu Children in Britain (with Robert Jackson) Trentham Books, 1993
Guru Nanak (with Gopinder Kaur) Bayeux Arts, 1999
The Religious Lives of Sikh Children: A Coventry based study, Department of Theology and Religious Studies, University of Leeds, 2000
Interfaith Pilgrims, Quaker Books, 2003
Intercultural Education: Ethnographic and religious approaches, Sussex Academic Press, 2004
Sikhism A Very Short Introduction, Oxford University Press, 2005; 2nd revised edn 2016
Pool of Life: The autobiography of a Punjabi agony aunt (with Kailash Puri), Sussex Academic Press, 2013
Making Nothing Happen: Five poets explore faith and spirituality (with Gavin D'Costa, Mark Pryce, Ruth Shelton and Nicola Slee) Ashgate, 2014
Sikh: Two centuries of western women's art and writing, Kashi House, 2022

Contact the author

Do contact me with any queries or comments although I may not always be able to answer them. My email address is:
eleanor.nesbitt@warwick.ac.uk

Also in this series

Quaker Quicks - Practical Mystics Quaker Faith in Action
Jennifer Kavanagh ISBN: 978-1-78904-279-5

Quaker Quicks - Hearing the Light The core of Quaker theology
Rhiannon Grant ISBN: 978-1-78904-504-8

*Quaker Quicks - In STEP with Quaker Testimony Simplicity, Truth,
Equality and Peace - inspired by Margaret Fell's writings Joanna
Godfrey Wood*
ISBN: 978-1-78904-577-2

*Quaker Quicks - Telling the Truth About God Quaker
approaches to theology*
Rhiannon Grant ISBN: 978-1-78904-081-4

*Quaker Quicks - Money and Soul Quaker Faith and Practice
and the Economy*
Pamela Haines ISBN: 978-1-78904-089-0

*Quaker Quicks - Hope and Witness in Dangerous Times Lessons
from the Quakers On Blending Faith, Daily Life, and Activism*
J. Brent Bill ISBN: 978-1-78904-619-9

*Quaker Quicks - In Search of Stillness Using a simple
meditation to find inner peace*
Joanna Godfrey Wood ISBN: 978-1-78904-707-3

CHRISTIAN ALTERNATIVE
BOOKS

THE NEW OPEN SPACES

Throughout the two thousand years of Christian tradition
there have been, and still are, groups and individuals that
exist in the margins and upon the edge of faith. But in
Christianity's contrapuntal history it has often been these
outcasts and pioneers that have forged contemporary
orthodoxy out of former radicalism as belief evolves to engage
with and encompass the ever-changing social and scientific
realities. Real faith lies not in the comfortable certainties of
the Orthodox, but somewhere in a half-glimpsed hinterland
on the dirt track to Emmaus, where the Death of God meets
the Resurrection, where the supernatural Christ meets the
historical Jesus, and where the revolution liberates both the
oppressed and the oppressors.

Welcome to Christian Alternative... a space at the edge where
the light shines through.
If you have enjoyed this book, why not tell other readers by
posting a review on your preferred book site.

Recent bestsellers from Christian Alternative are:

Bread Not Stones
The Autobiography of An Eventful
Life Una Kroll
The spiritual autobiography of a truly remarkable woman
and a history of the struggle for ordination in the Church of
England.
Paperback: 978-1-78279-804-0 ebook: 978-1-78279-805-7

The Quaker Way
A Rediscovery
Rex Ambler
Although fairly well known, Quakerism is not well
understood. The purpose of this book is to explain how
Quakerism works as a spiritual practice.
Paperback: 978-1-78099-657-8 ebook: 978-1-78099-658-5

Blue Sky God
The Evolution of Science and Christianity
Don MacGregor
Quantum consciousness, morphic fields and blue-sky thinking
about God and Jesus the Christ.
Paperback: 978-1-84694-937-1 ebook: 978-1-84694-938-8

Celtic Wheel of the Year
Tess Ward
An original and inspiring selection of prayers combining
Christian and Celtic Pagan traditions, and interweaving their
calendars into a single pattern of prayer for every morning and
night of the year.
Paperback: 978-1-90504-795-6

Christian Atheist
Belonging without Believing
Brian Mountford
Christian Atheists don't believe in God but miss him:
especially the transcendent beauty of his music, language,
ethics, and community.
Paperback: 978-1-84694-439-0 ebook: 978-1-84694-929-6

Compassion Or Apocalypse?
A Comprehensible Guide to the Thoughts of René Girard
James Warren
How René Girard changes the way we think about God and
the Bible, and its relevance for our apocalypse-threatened
world.
Paperback: 978-1-78279-073-0 ebook: 978-1-78279-072-3

Diary Of A Gay Priest
The Tightrope Walker
Rev. Dr. Malcolm Johnson
Full of anecdotes and amusing stories, but the Church is still a
dangerous place for a gay priest.
Paperback: 978-1-78279-002-0 ebook: 978-1-78099-999-9

Readers of ebooks can buy or view any of these bestsellers by
clicking on the live link in the title. Most titles are published
in paperback and as an ebook. Paperbacks are available in
traditional bookshops. Both print and ebook formats are
available online.

Find more titles and sign up to our readers' newsletter at
http://www.johnhuntpublishing.com/christianity Follow us on
Facebook at https://www.facebook.com/ChristianAlternative